Exploring Jessica

An Artistic Exploration of One Female Form

Standard Edition

By Gary D. Melton

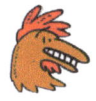

Goofy Rooster Publishing
Wylie, Texas
www.goofyrooster-publishing.com

Exploring Jessica
An Artistic Exploration of One Female Form
By Gary D. Melton

Goofy Rooster Publishing   PO Box 2904 Wylie, Texas 75098
www.goofyrooster-publishing.com

ISBN-10: 0-9843940-2-8

ISBN-13: 978-0-9843940-2-9

Standard Edition

Introduction

I was trying to come up with a concept for a new book the other day, and as often happens - one just wouldn't come to me when I tried to will it in to being. A few days later, when I wasn't thinking about it - a thought (no, really a memory) settled into my brain.

I'm not sure what triggered the memory, but I thought about a woman from my past and remembered what it was like to be intimate with her for the first time. It was just a short leap from there to recall other women from my past, and what it was like to be with them for the first time. I remembered the feelings and emotions that I felt the first time I saw them unclothed. I remembered the feelings and emotions I felt the first time I explored their bodies.

From that small memory grew the idea for this book - to completely and totally "explore" one female form. I wanted to create photos that captured that experience - an experience that many people have had and enjoyed. I hope I've at least come close, and I sincerely hope you enjoy my "vision".

I'd like to say "thanks" to the amazing model who adorns these pages - Jessica. She was wonderfully open to my ideas and direction for the images you see here.

Gary Melton

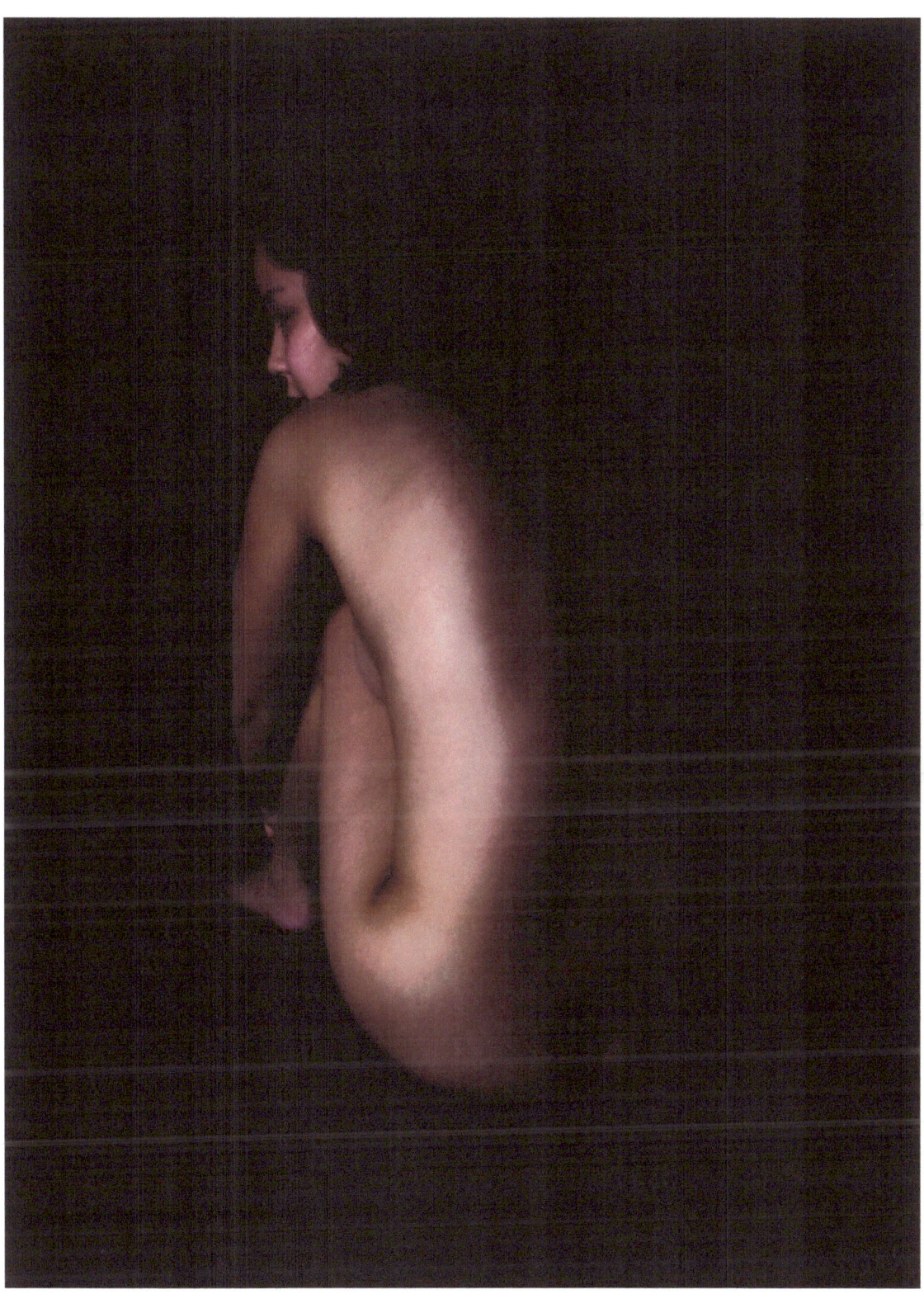

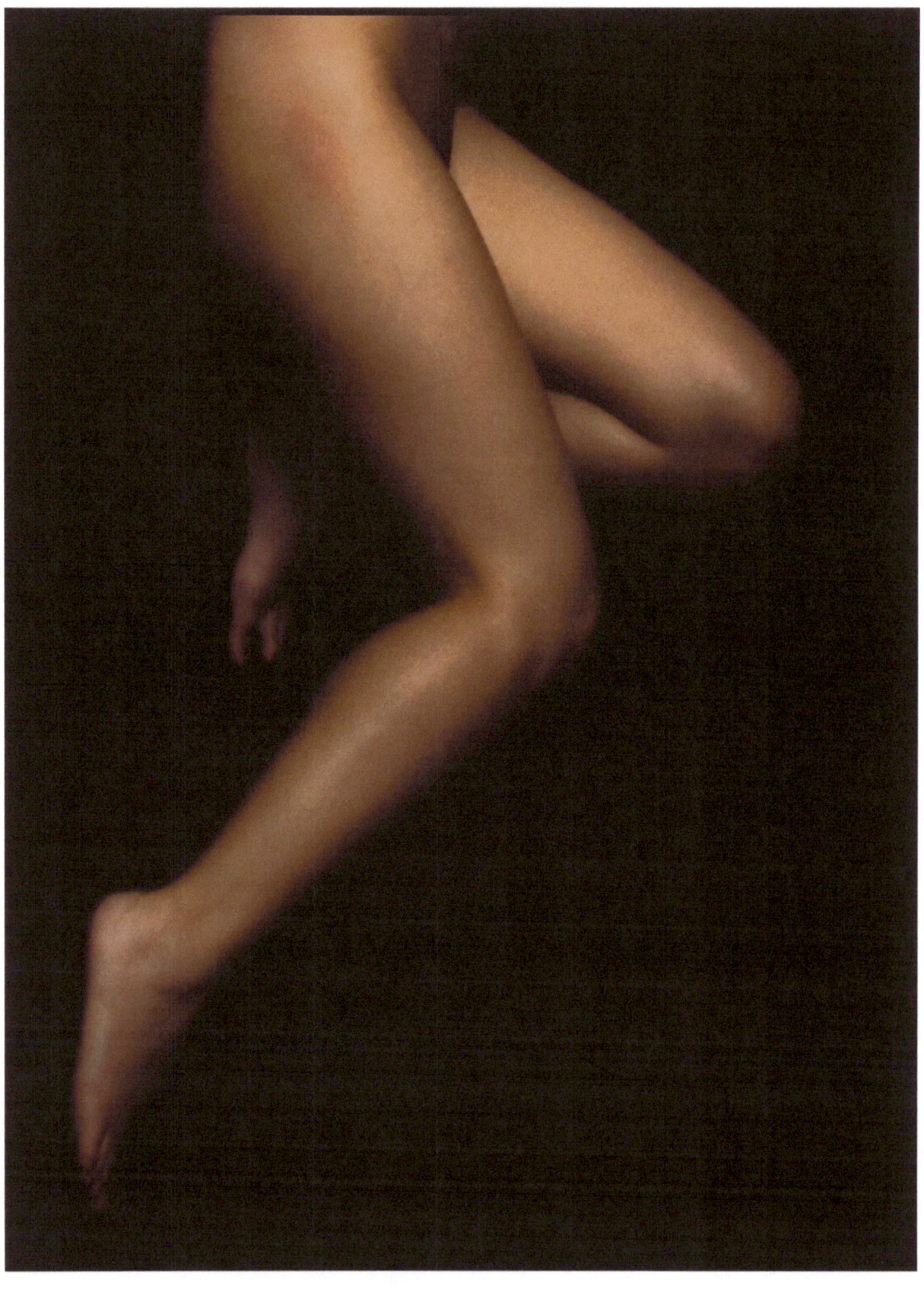

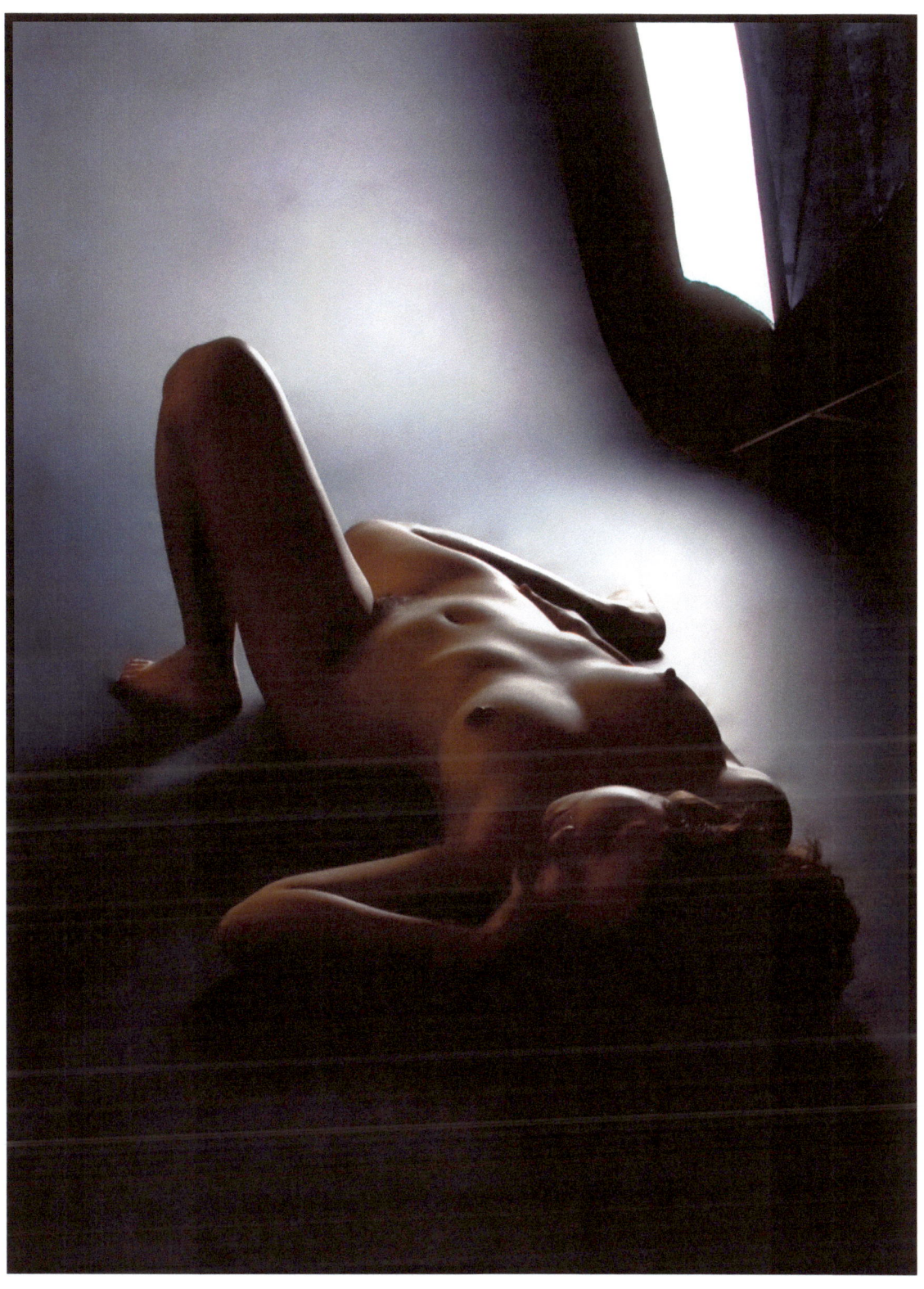

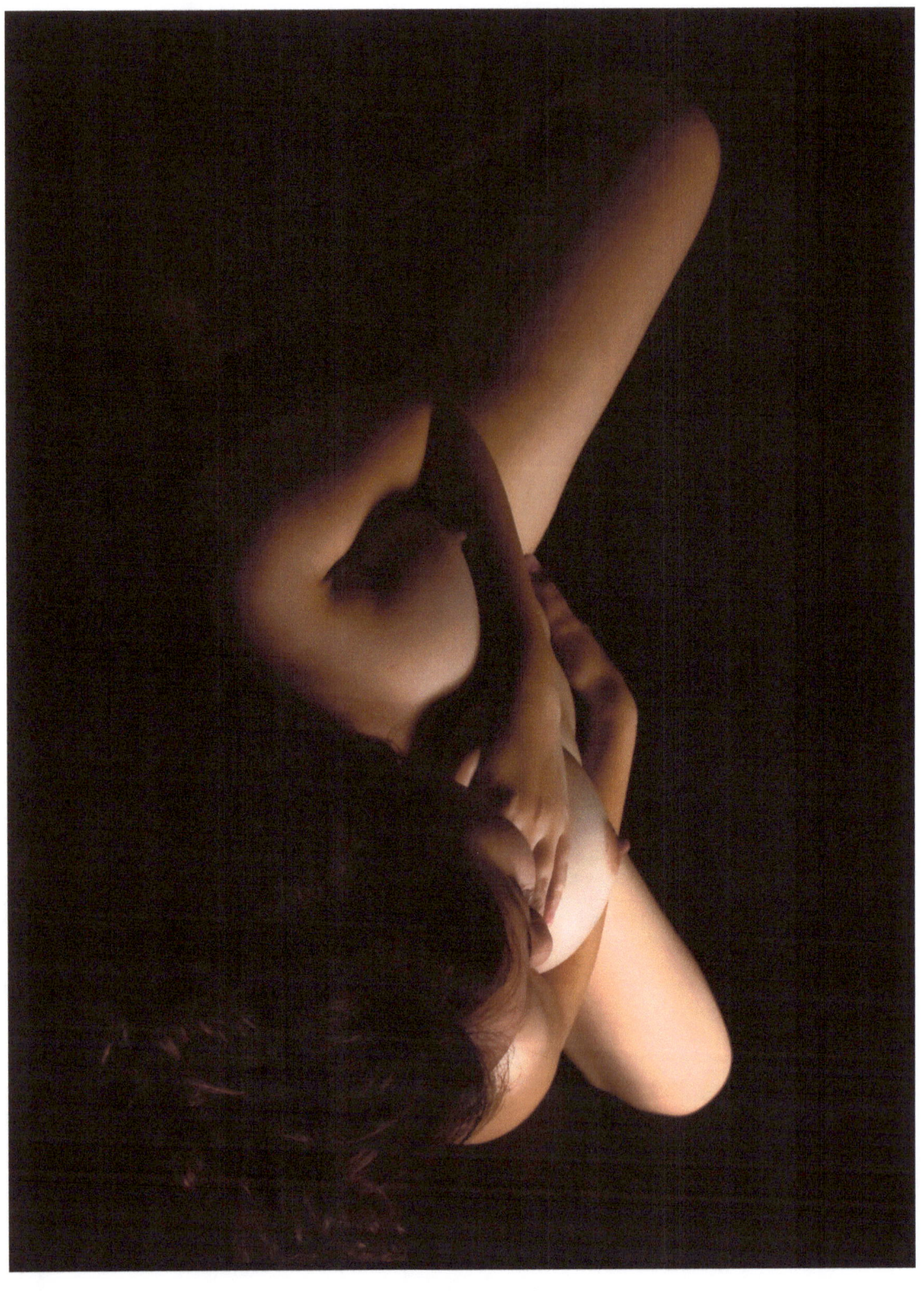

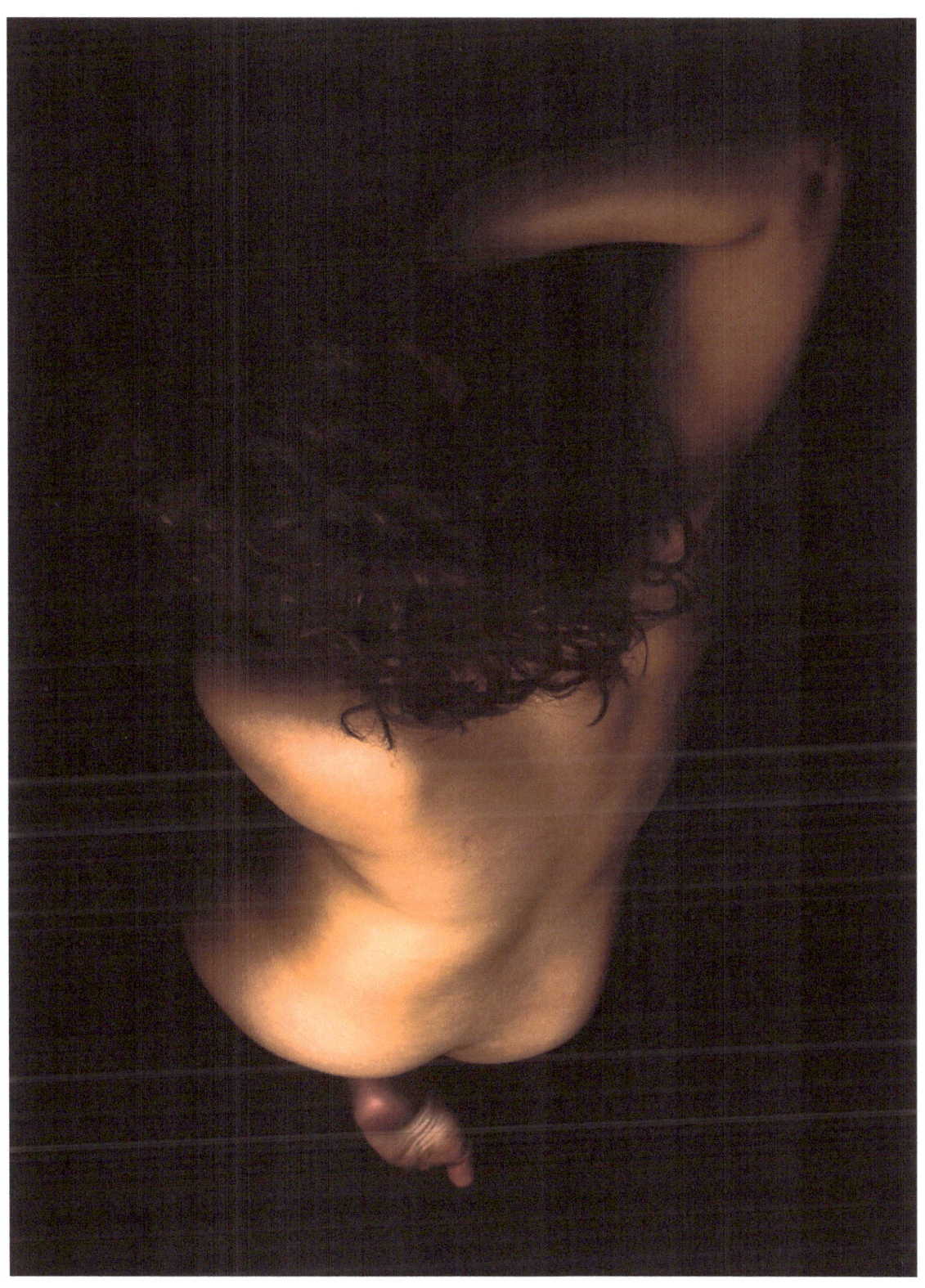

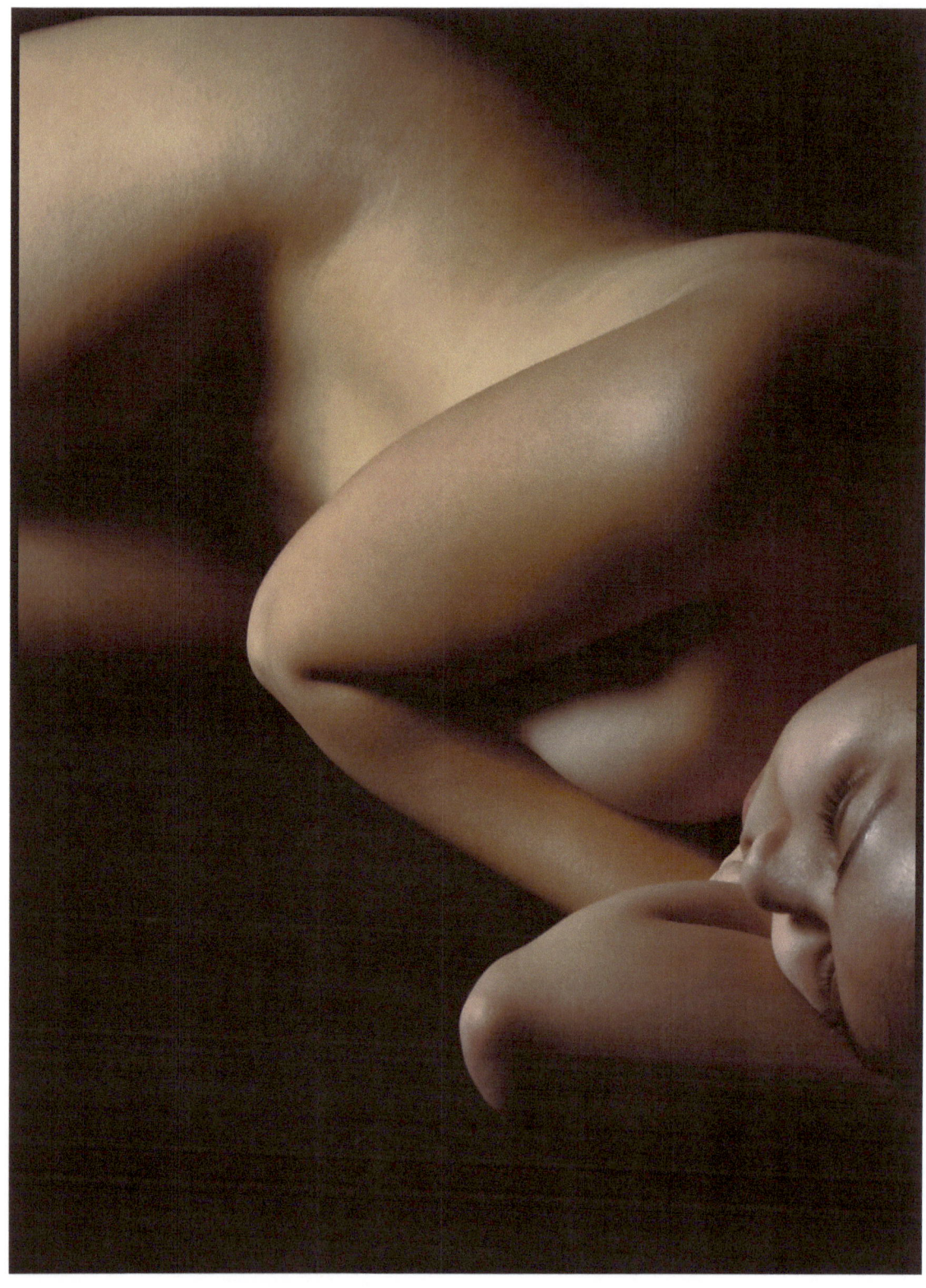

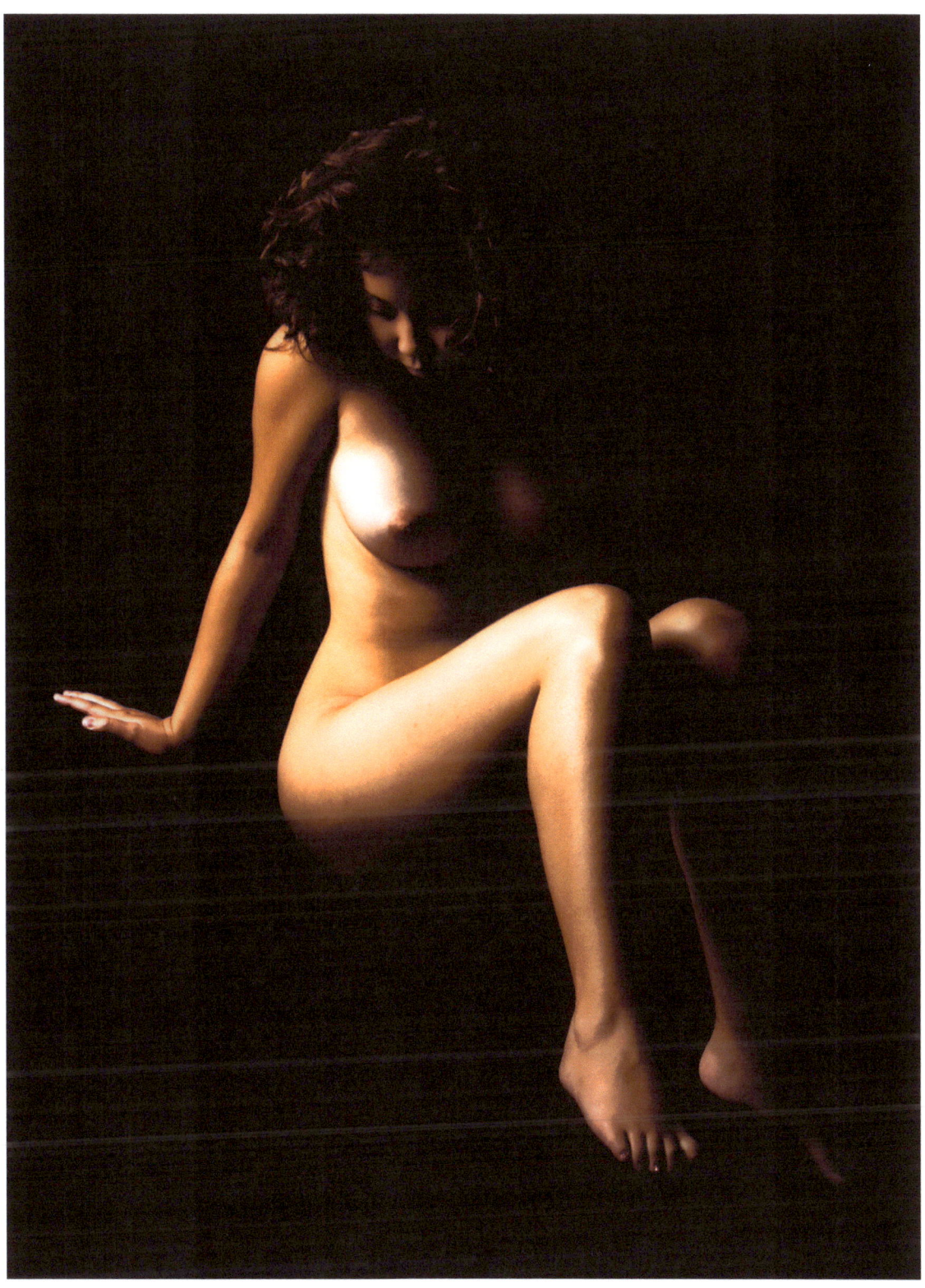

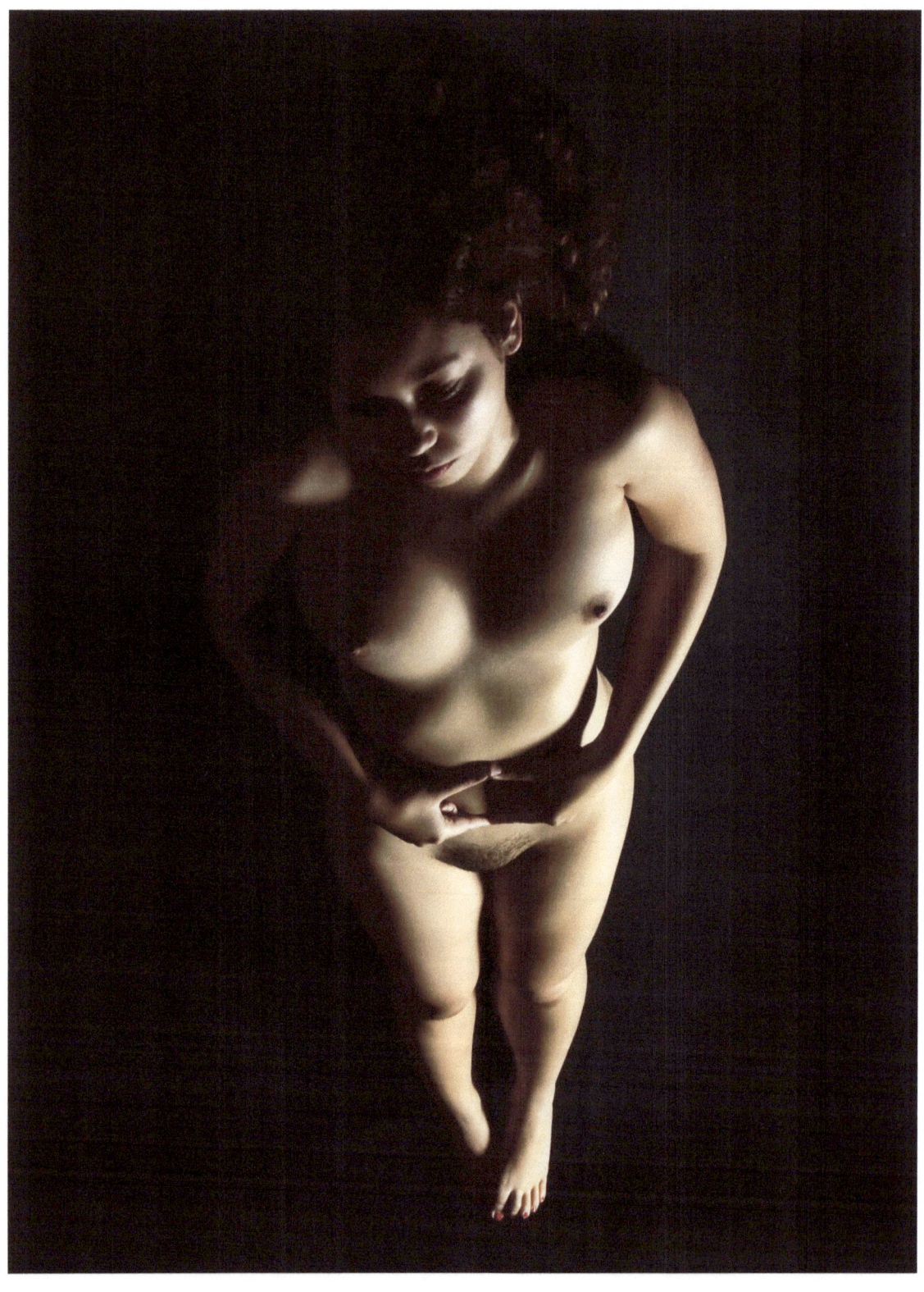

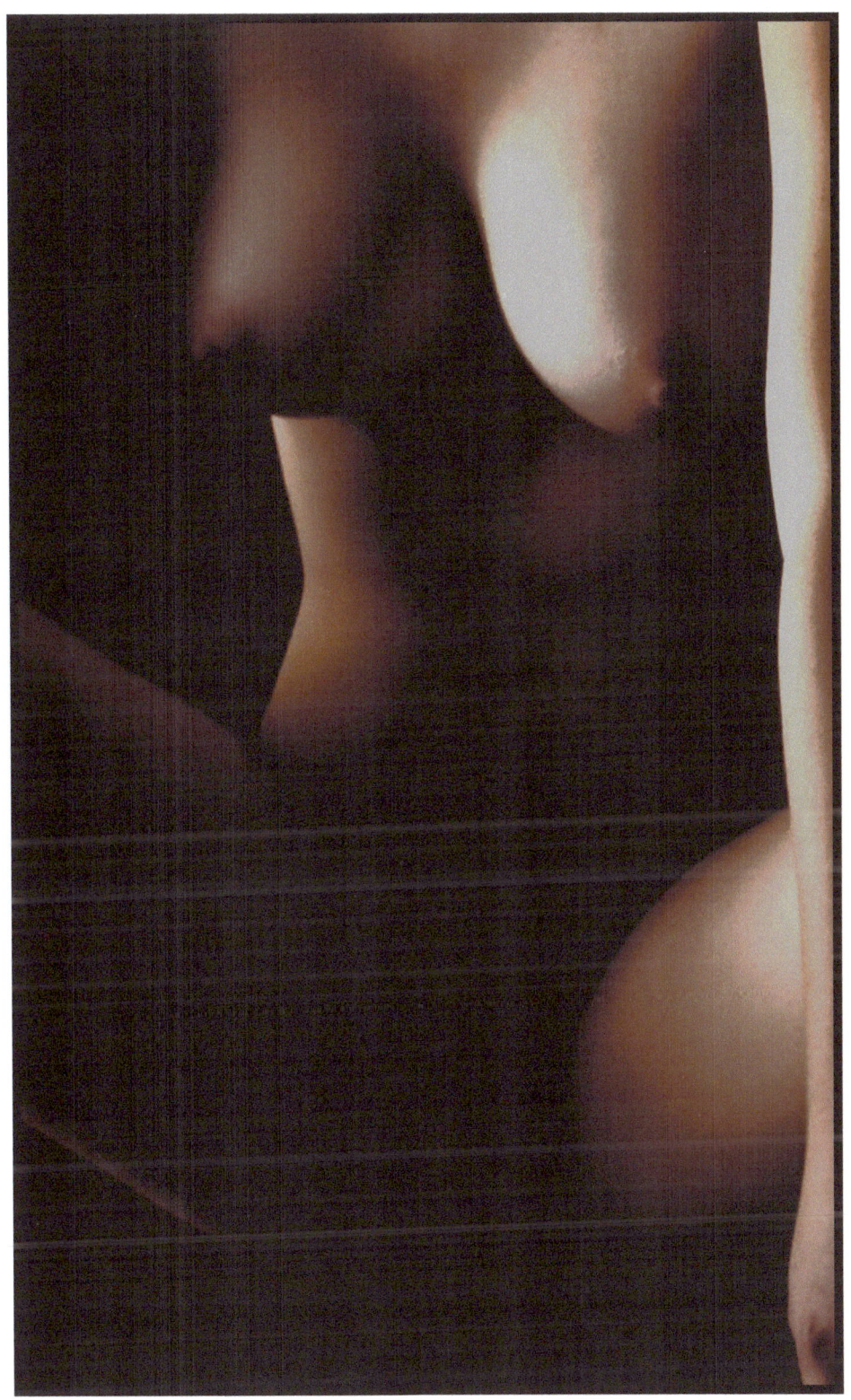

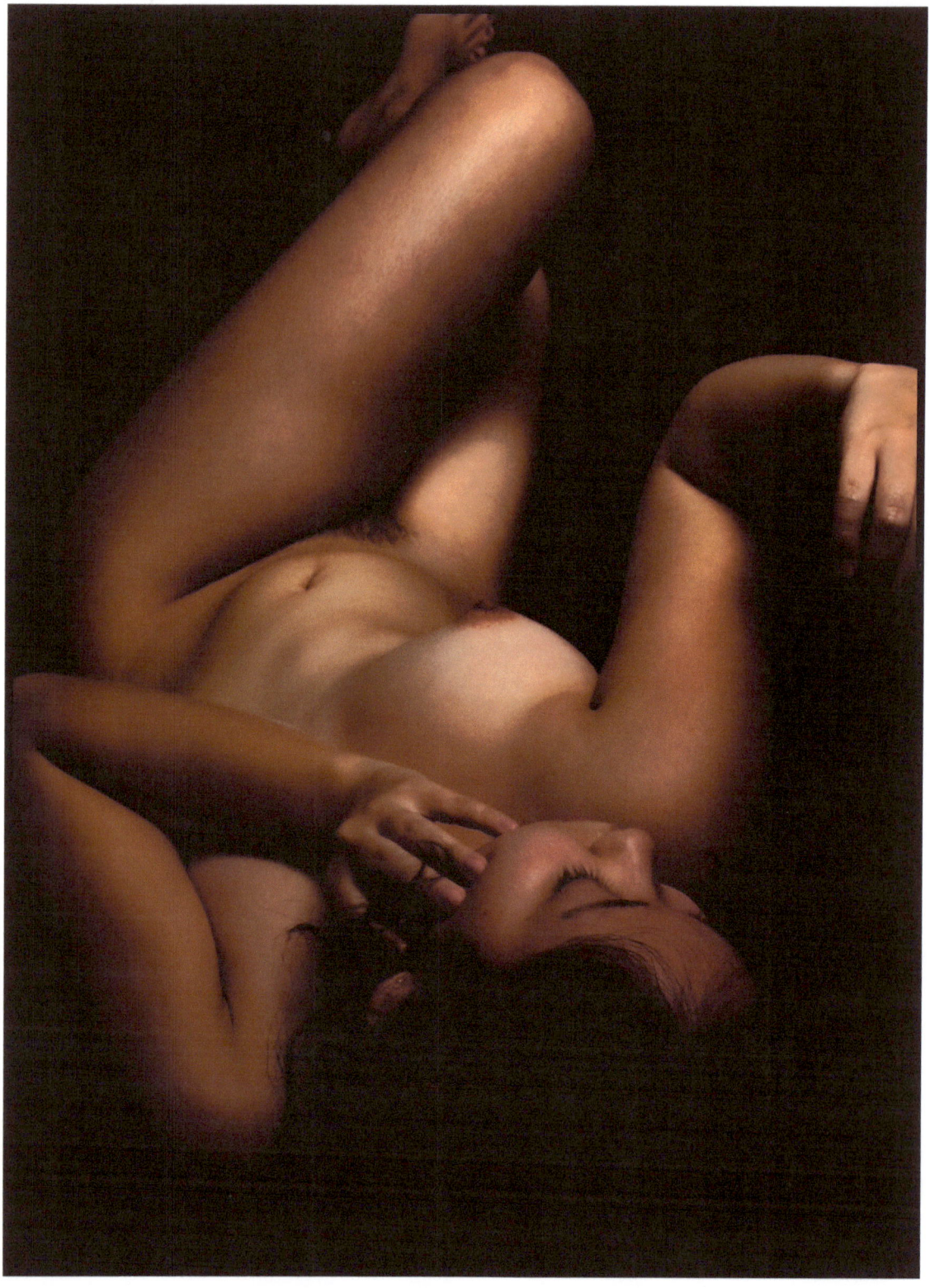

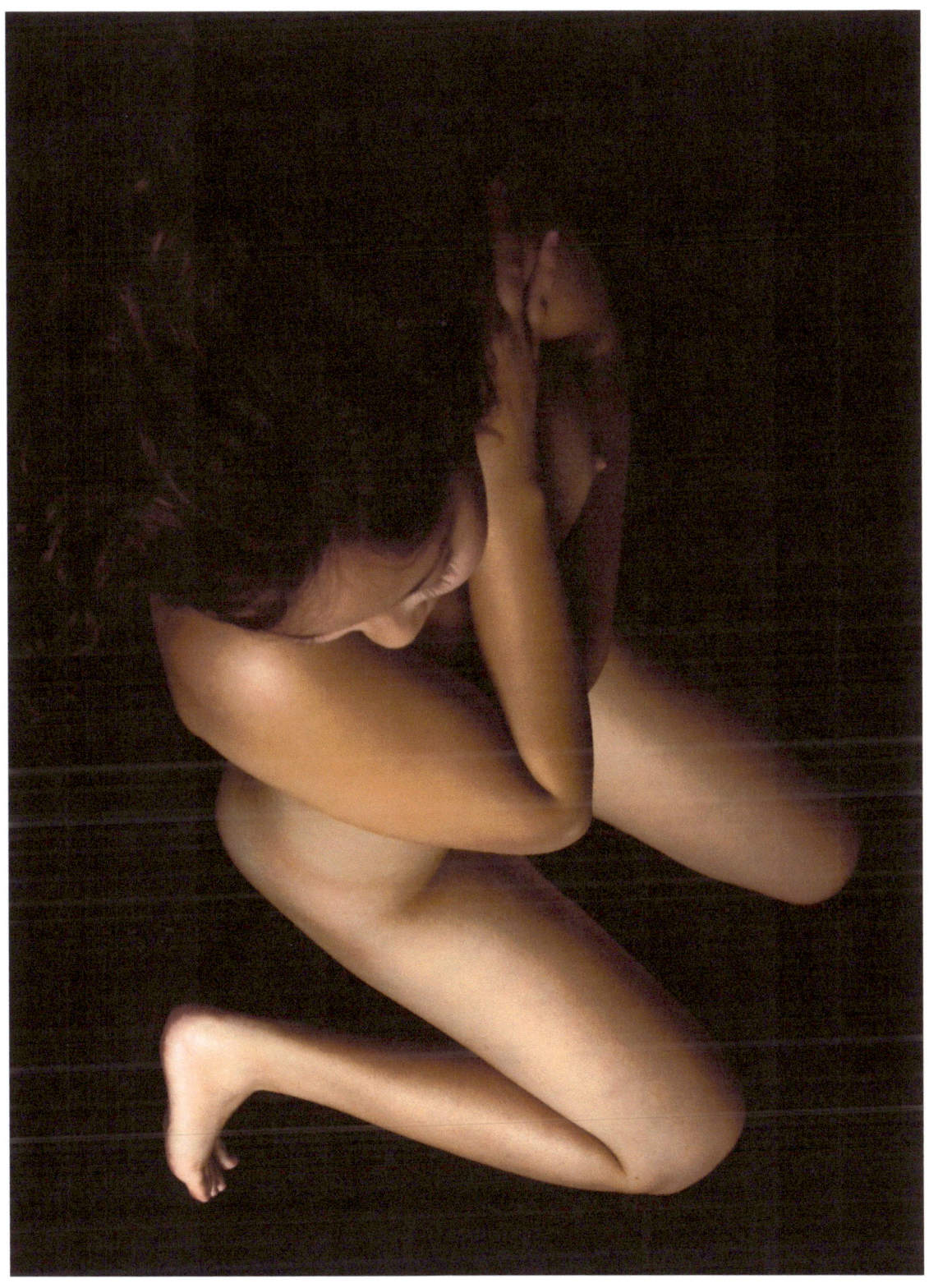

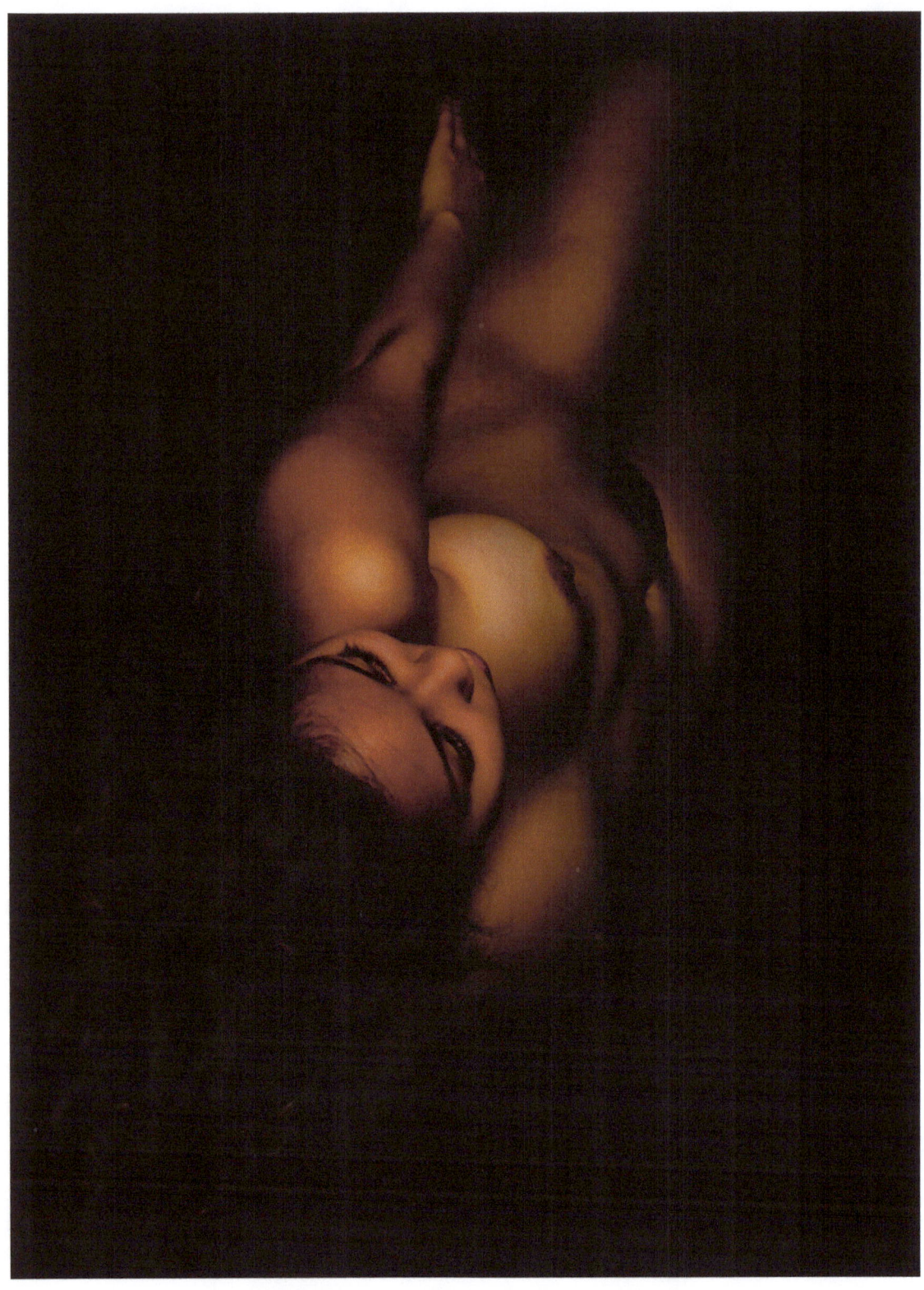

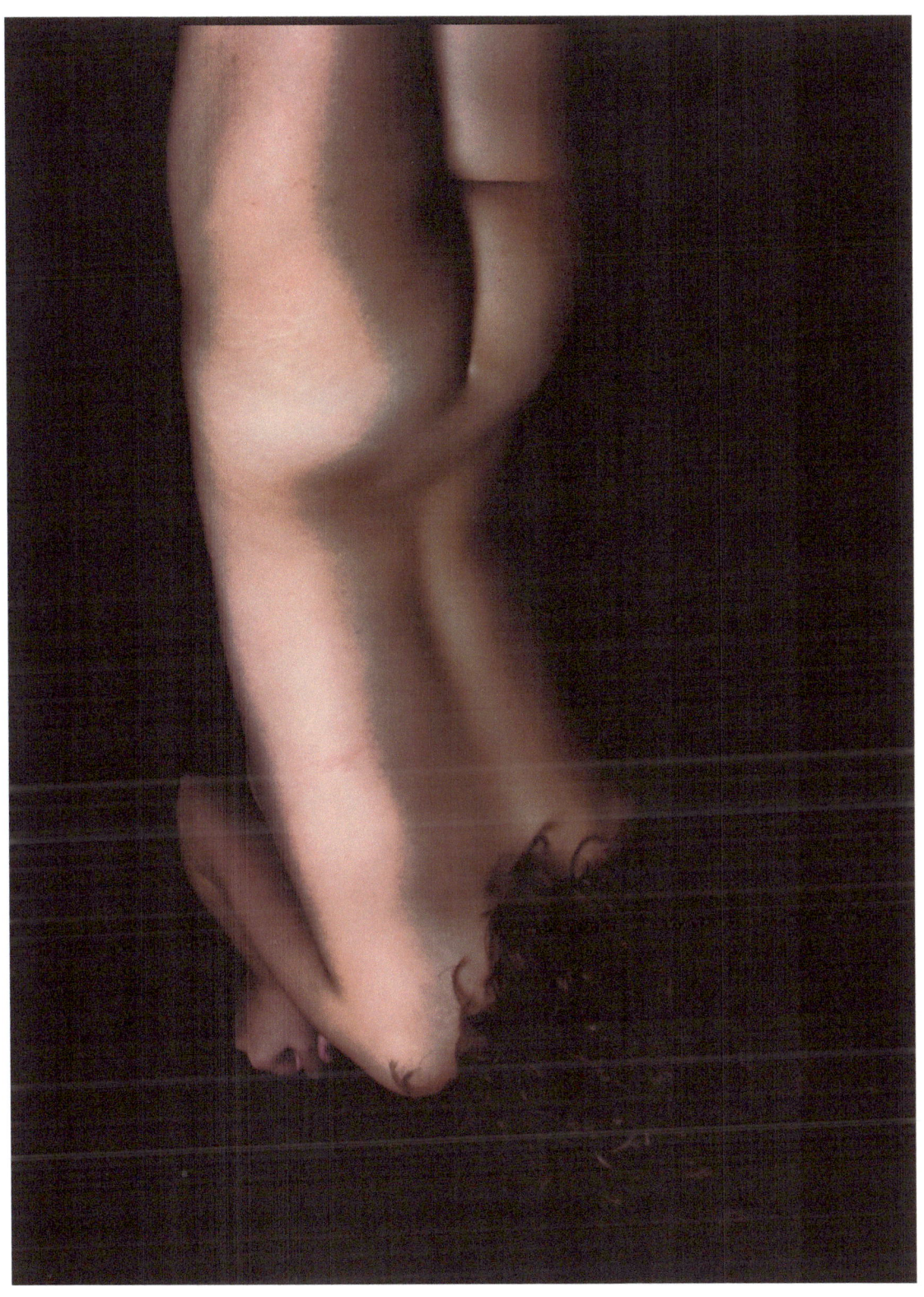

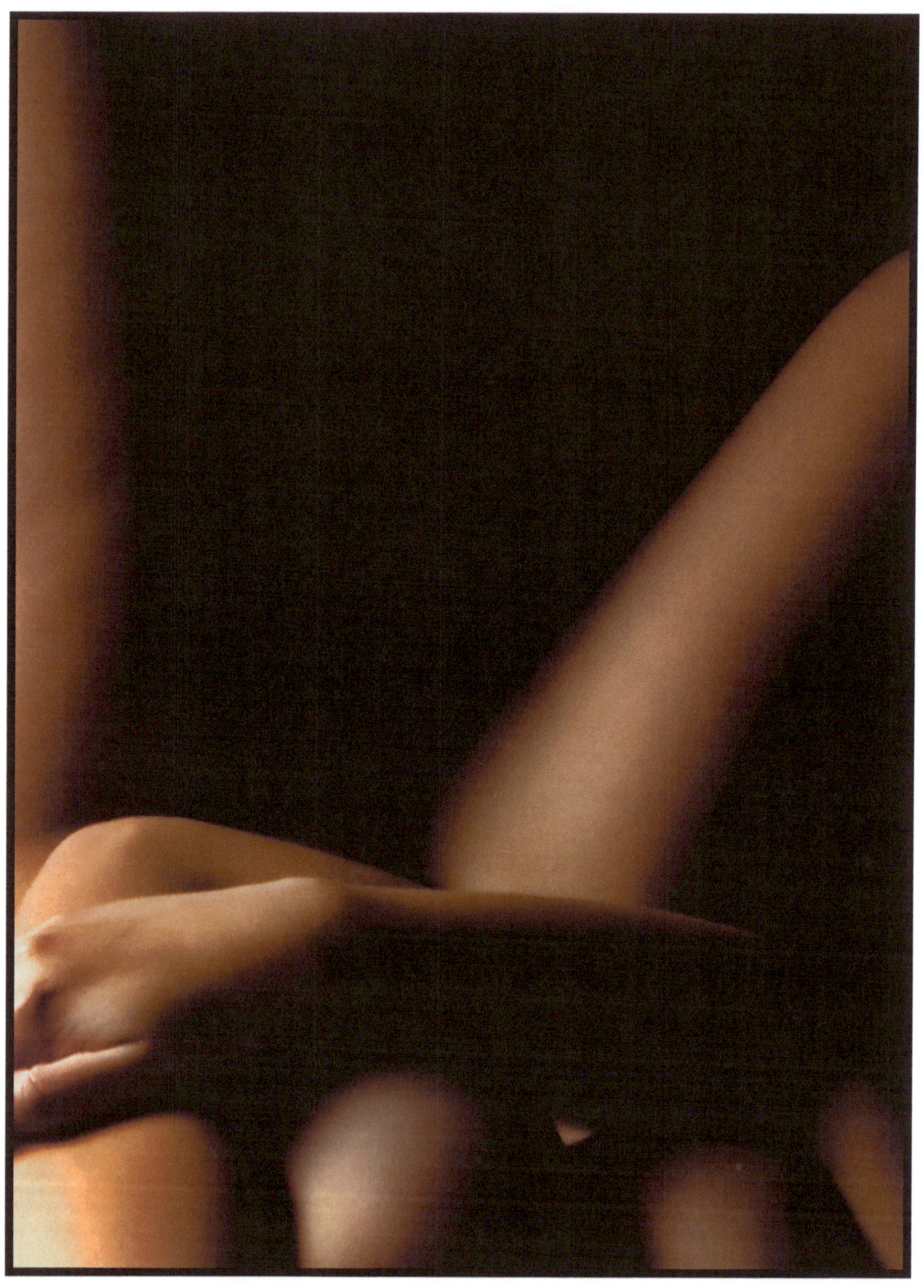

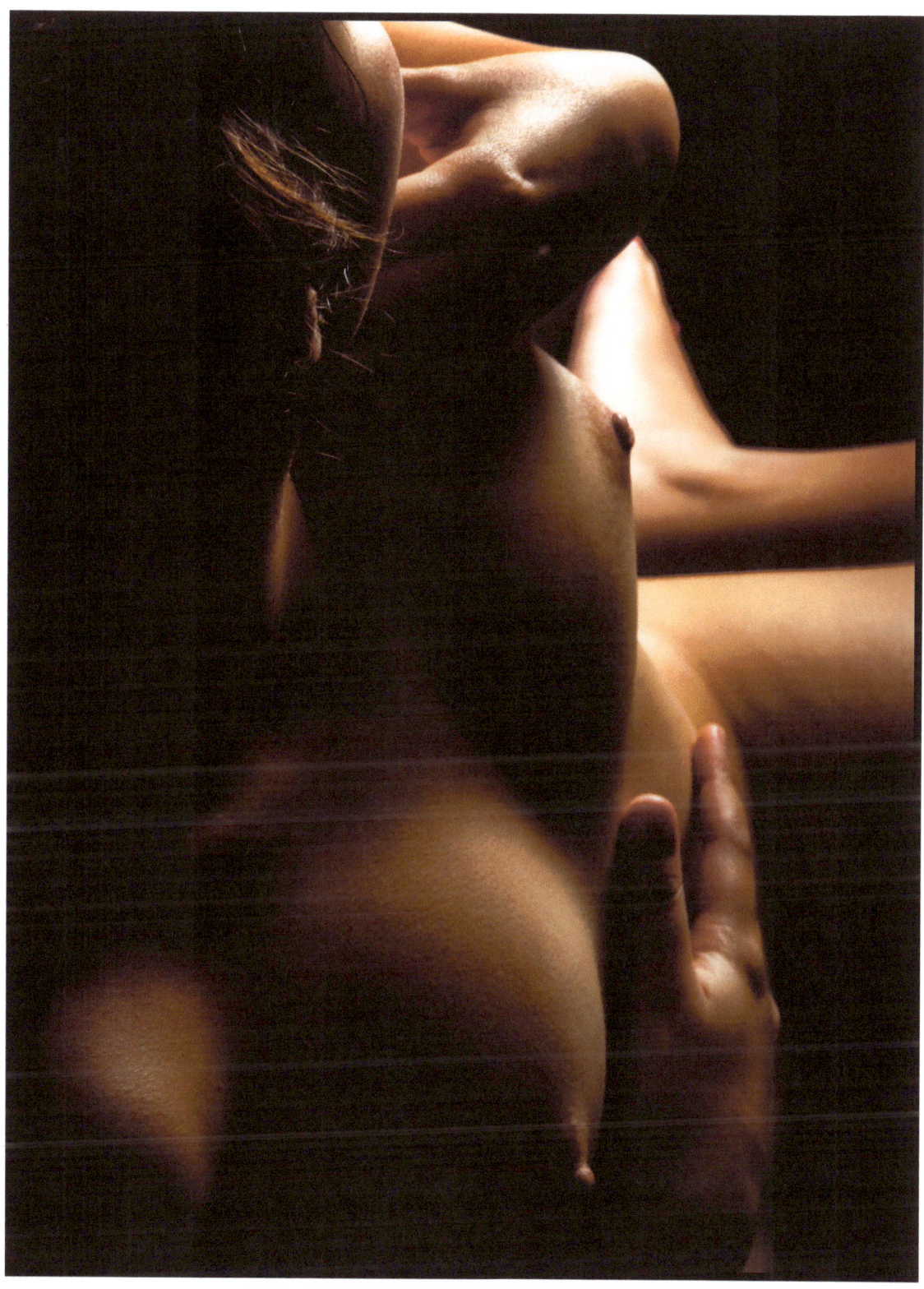

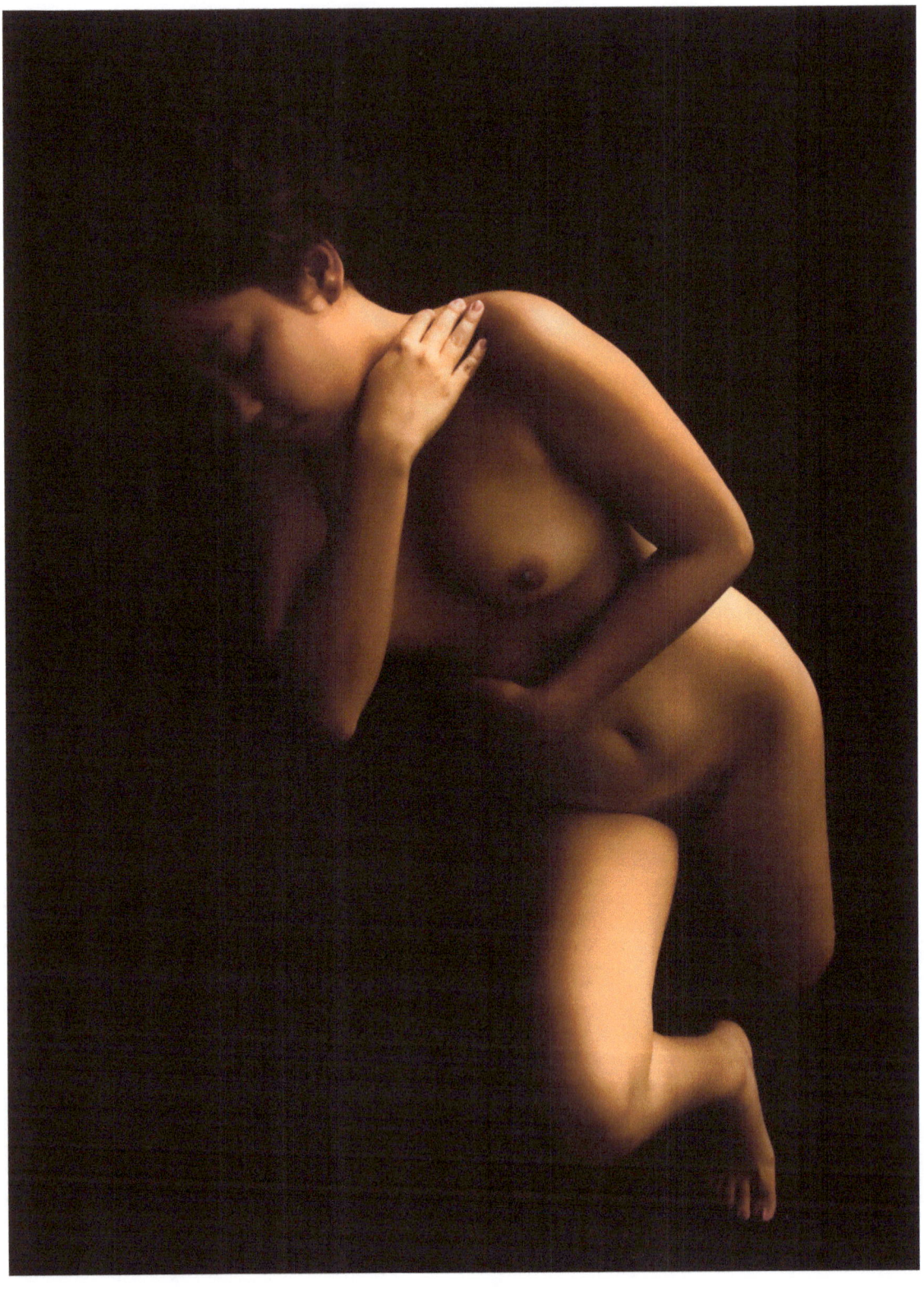

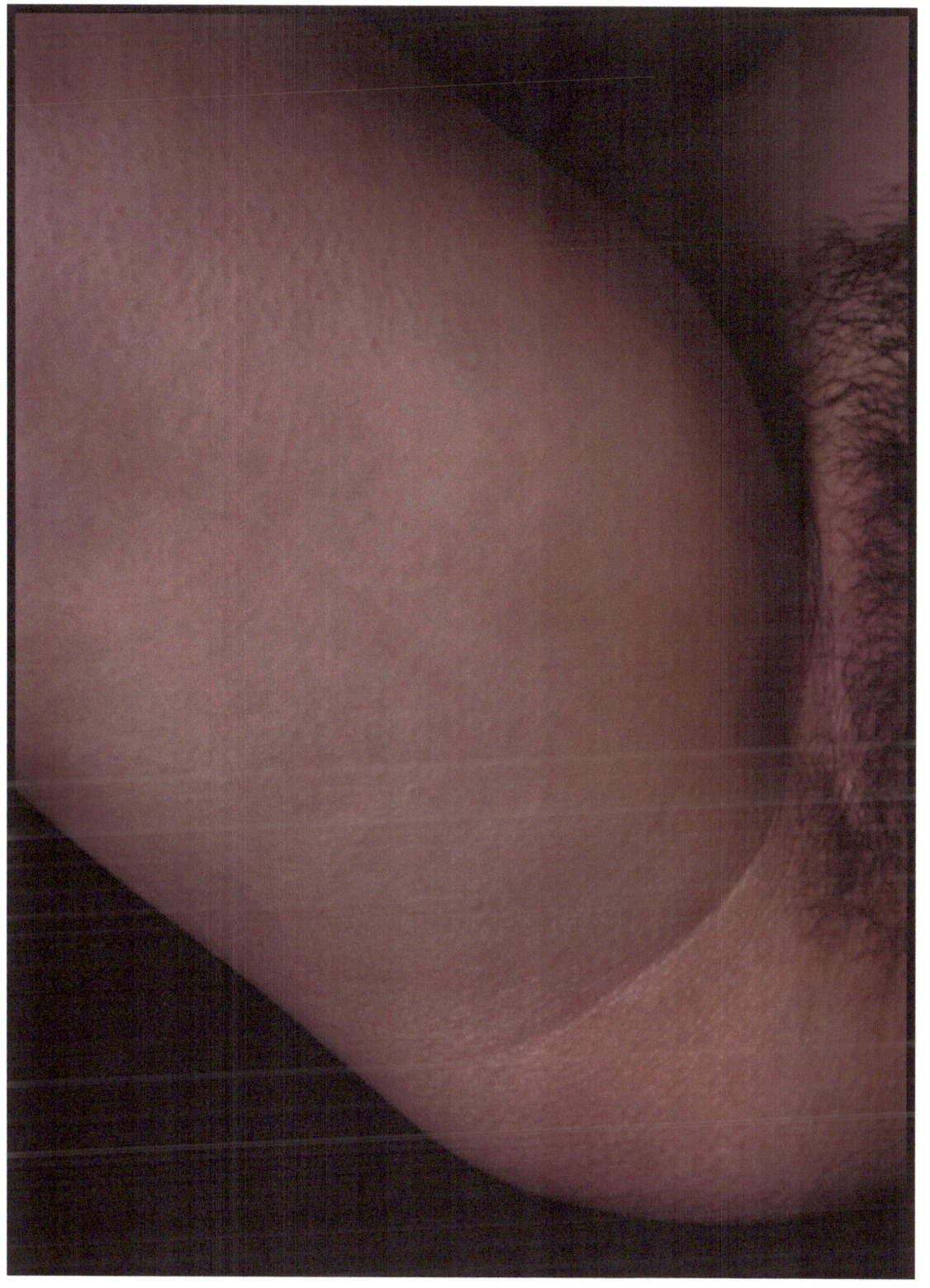

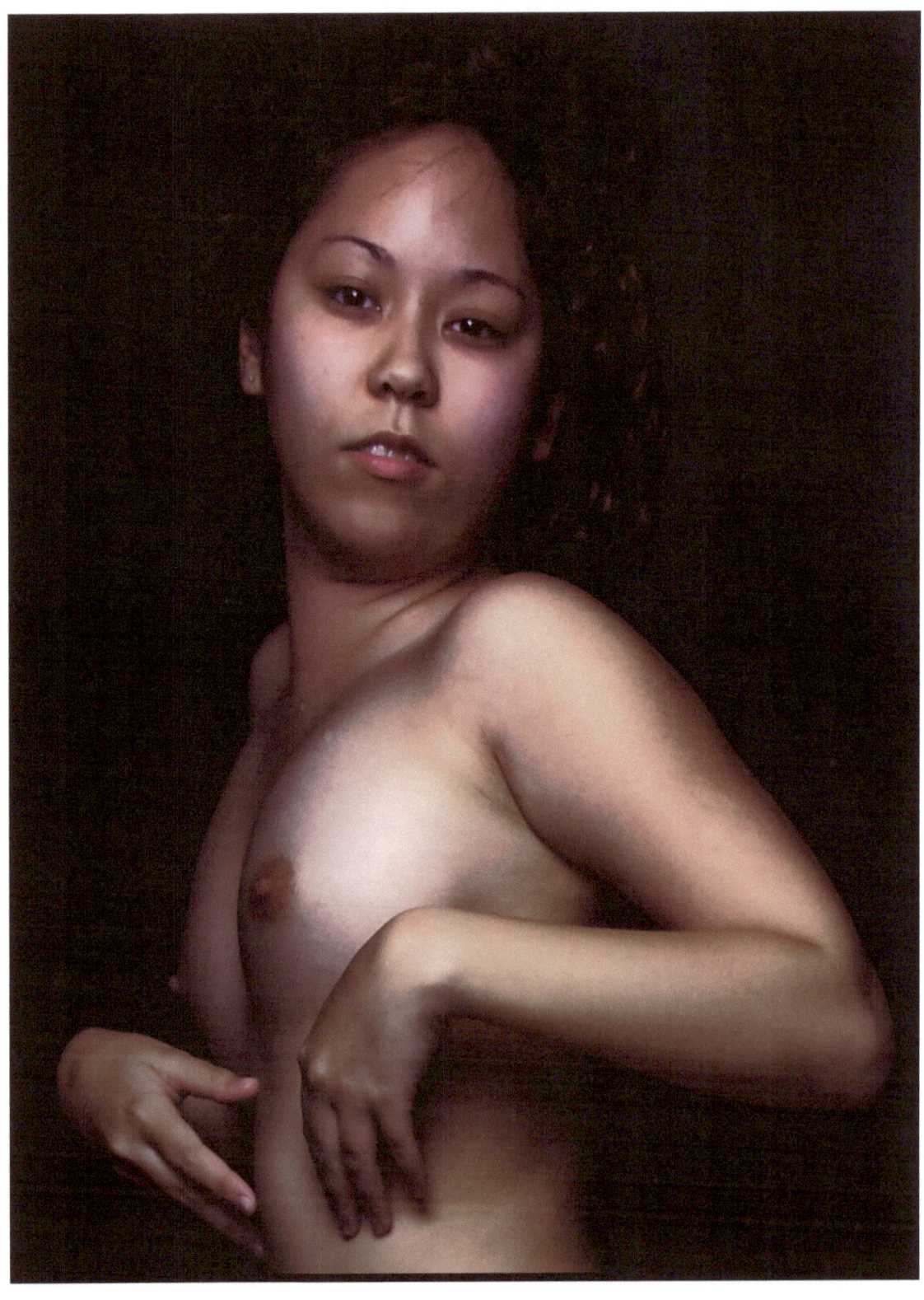

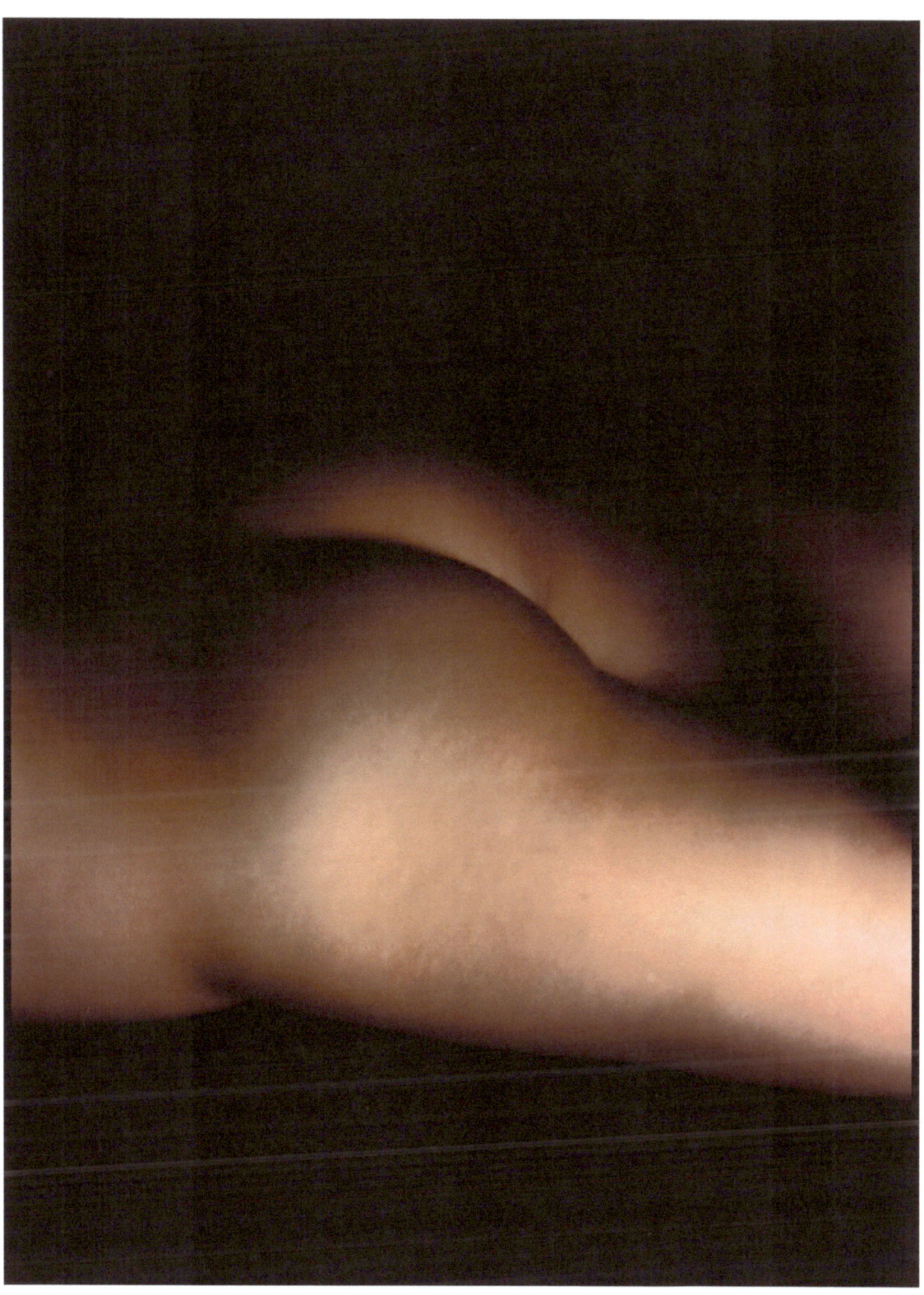

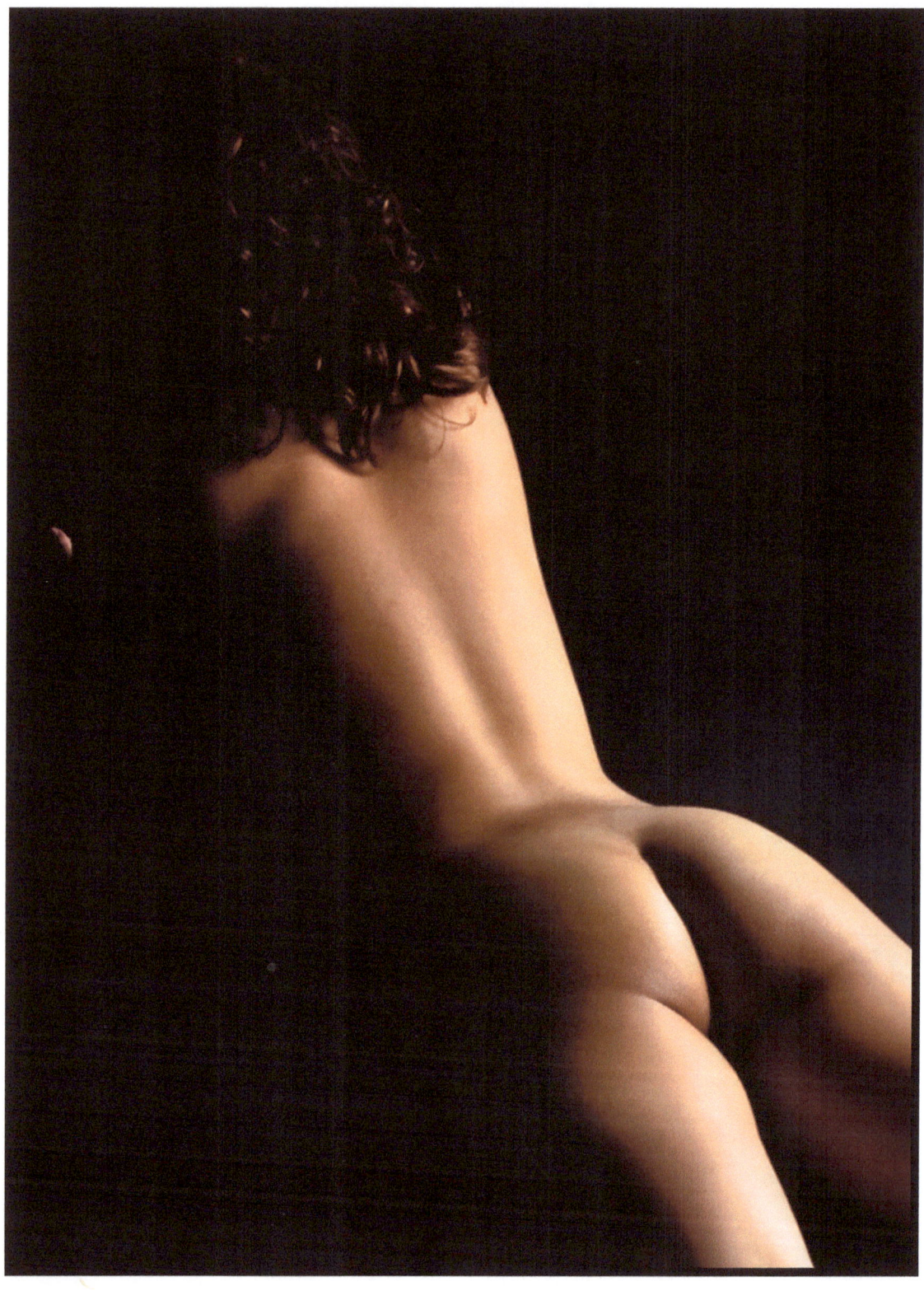

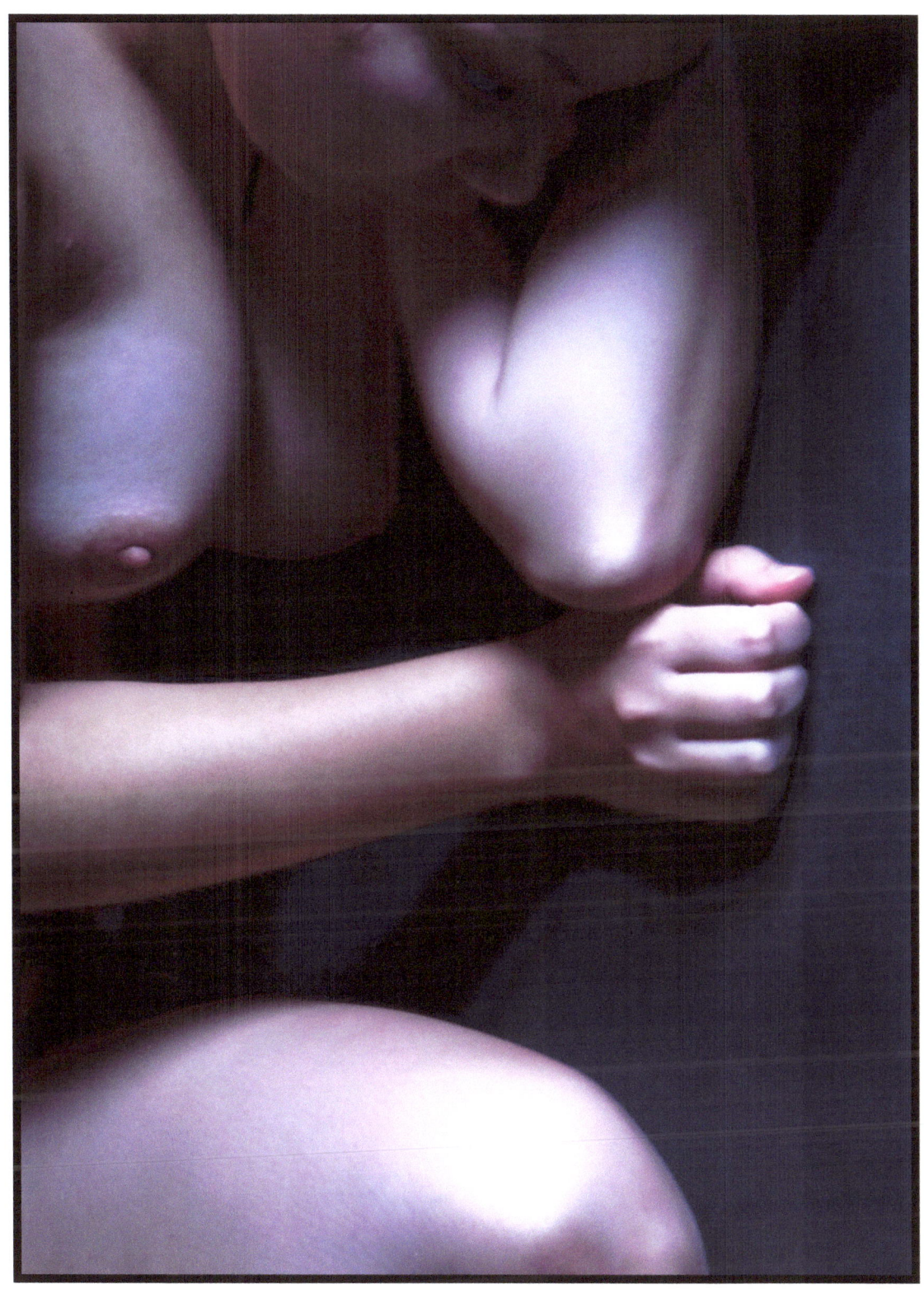

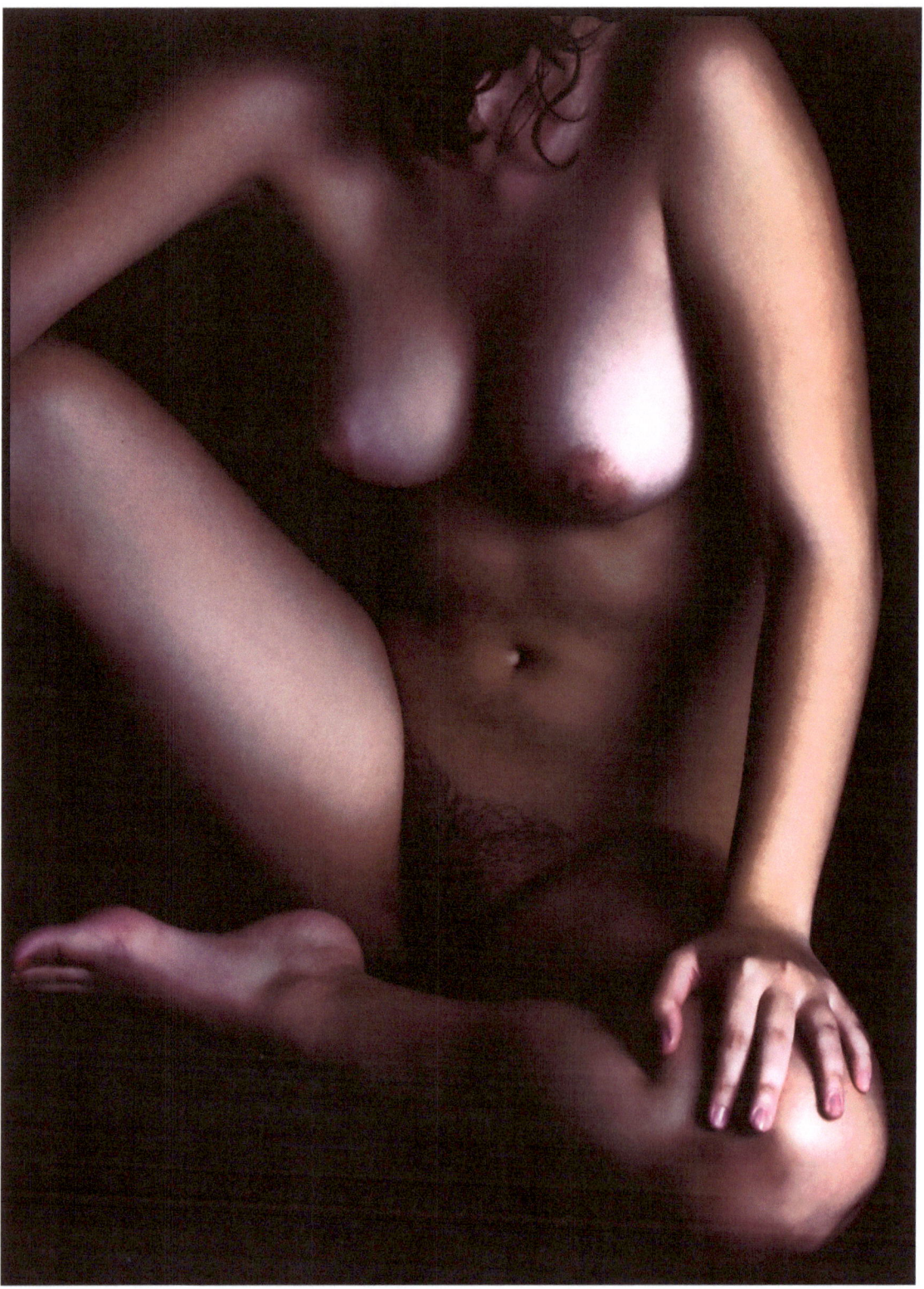

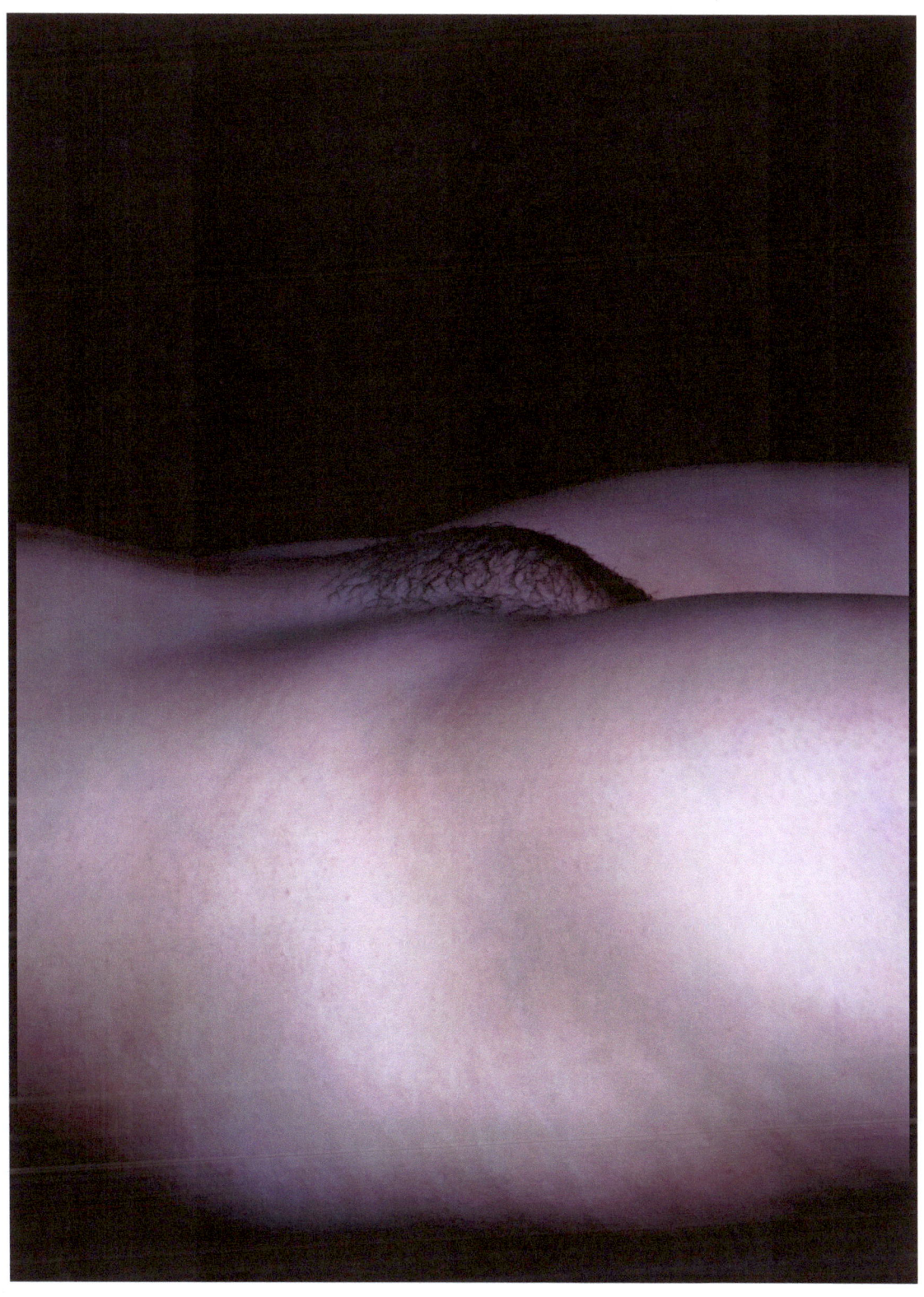

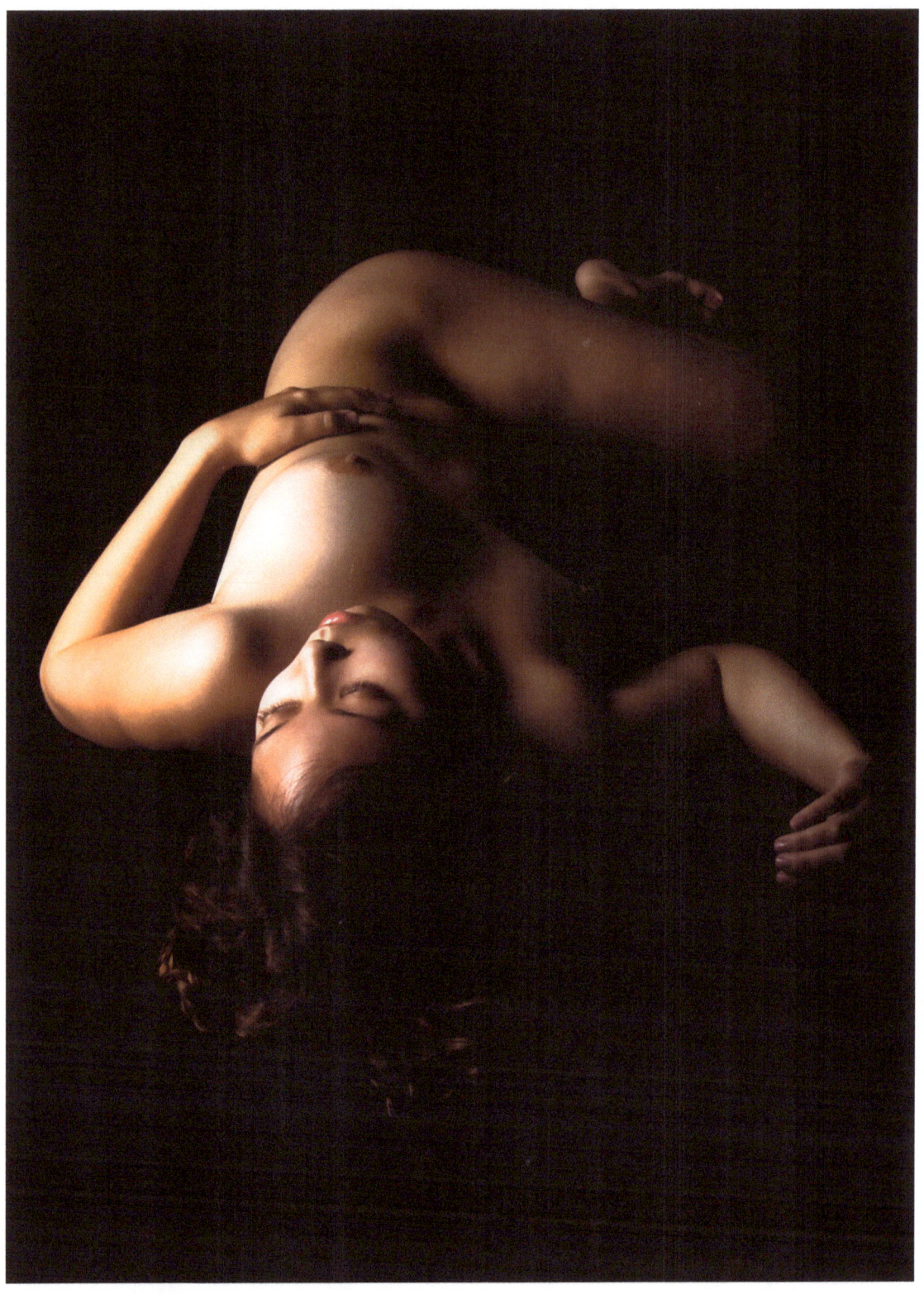

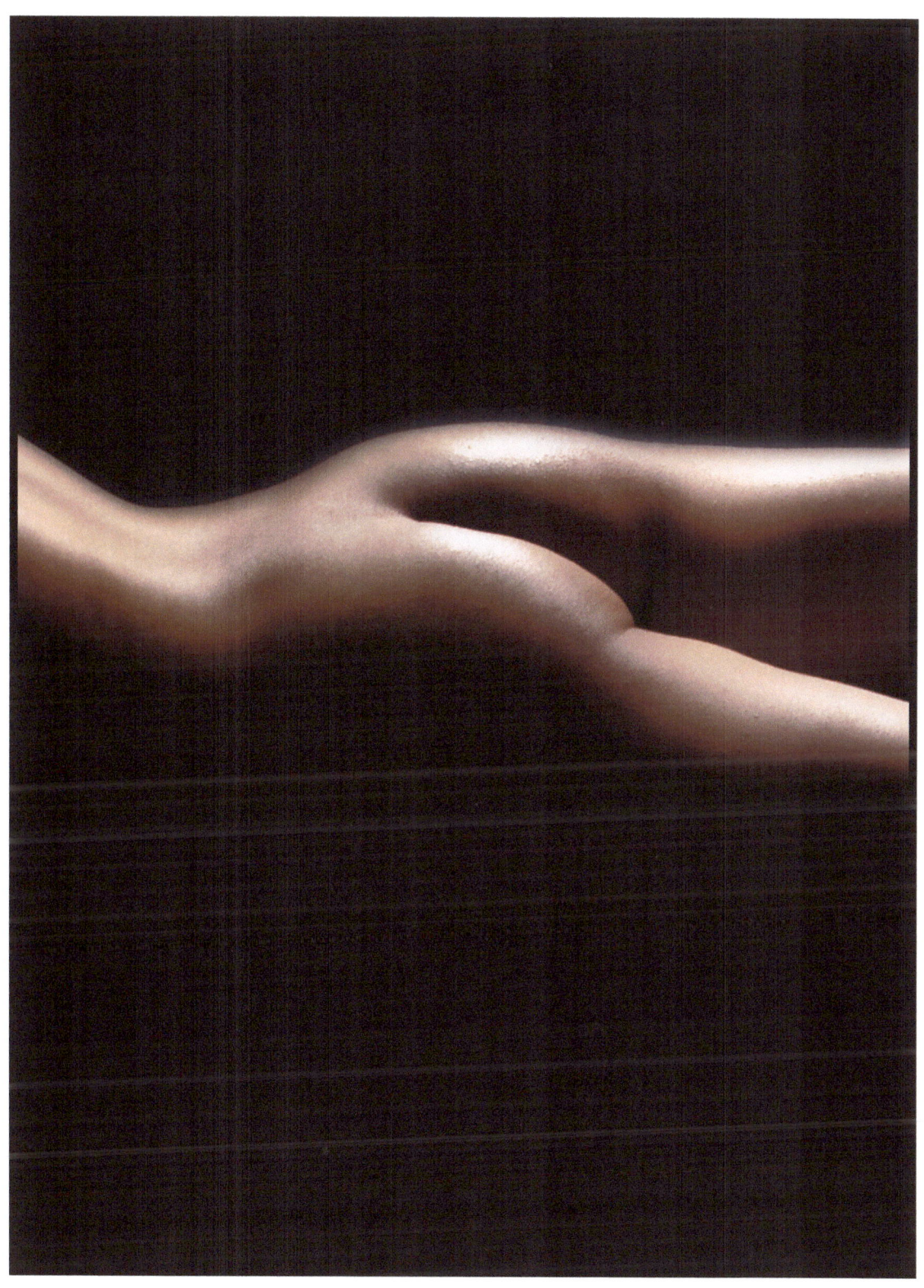

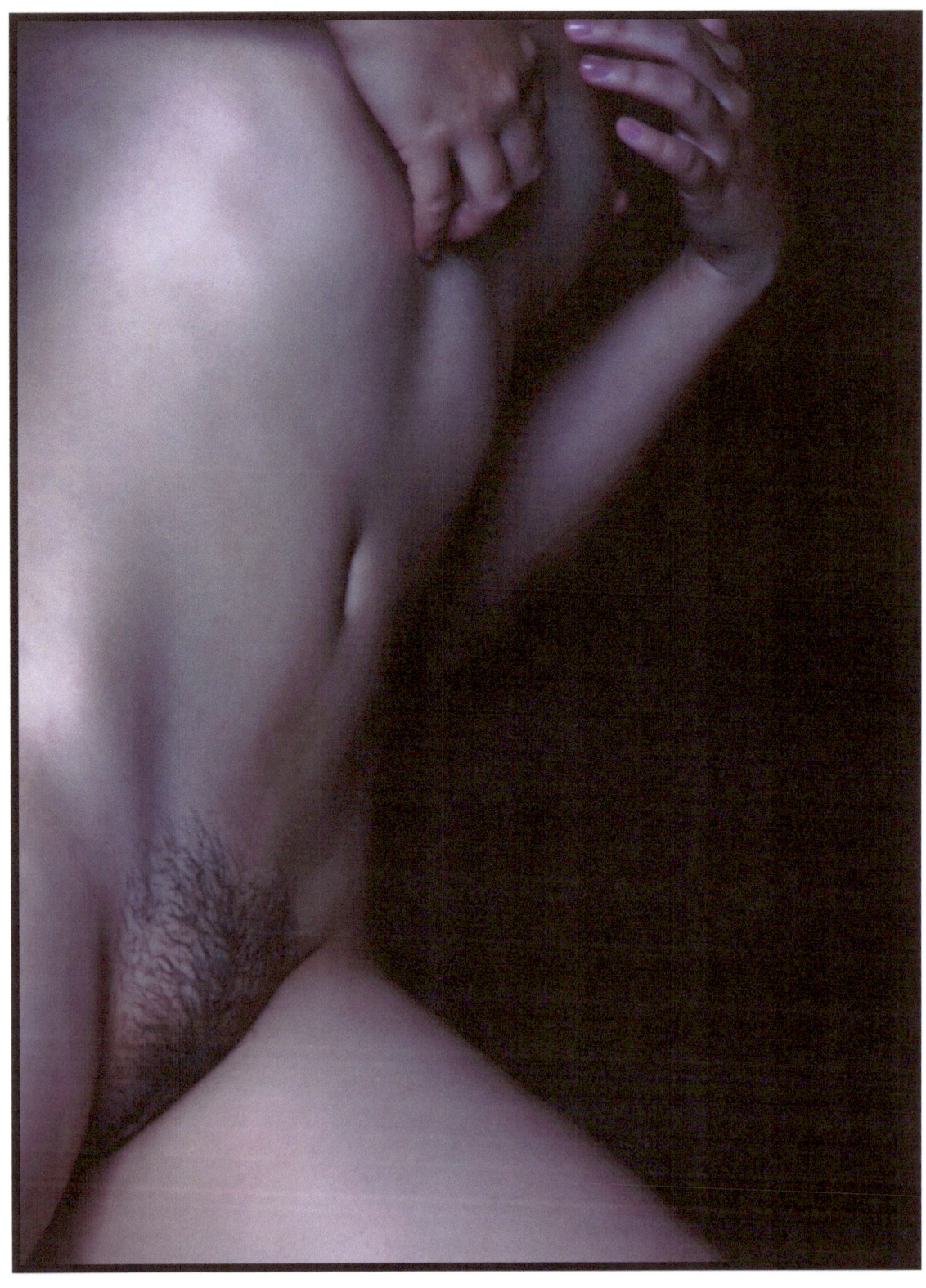

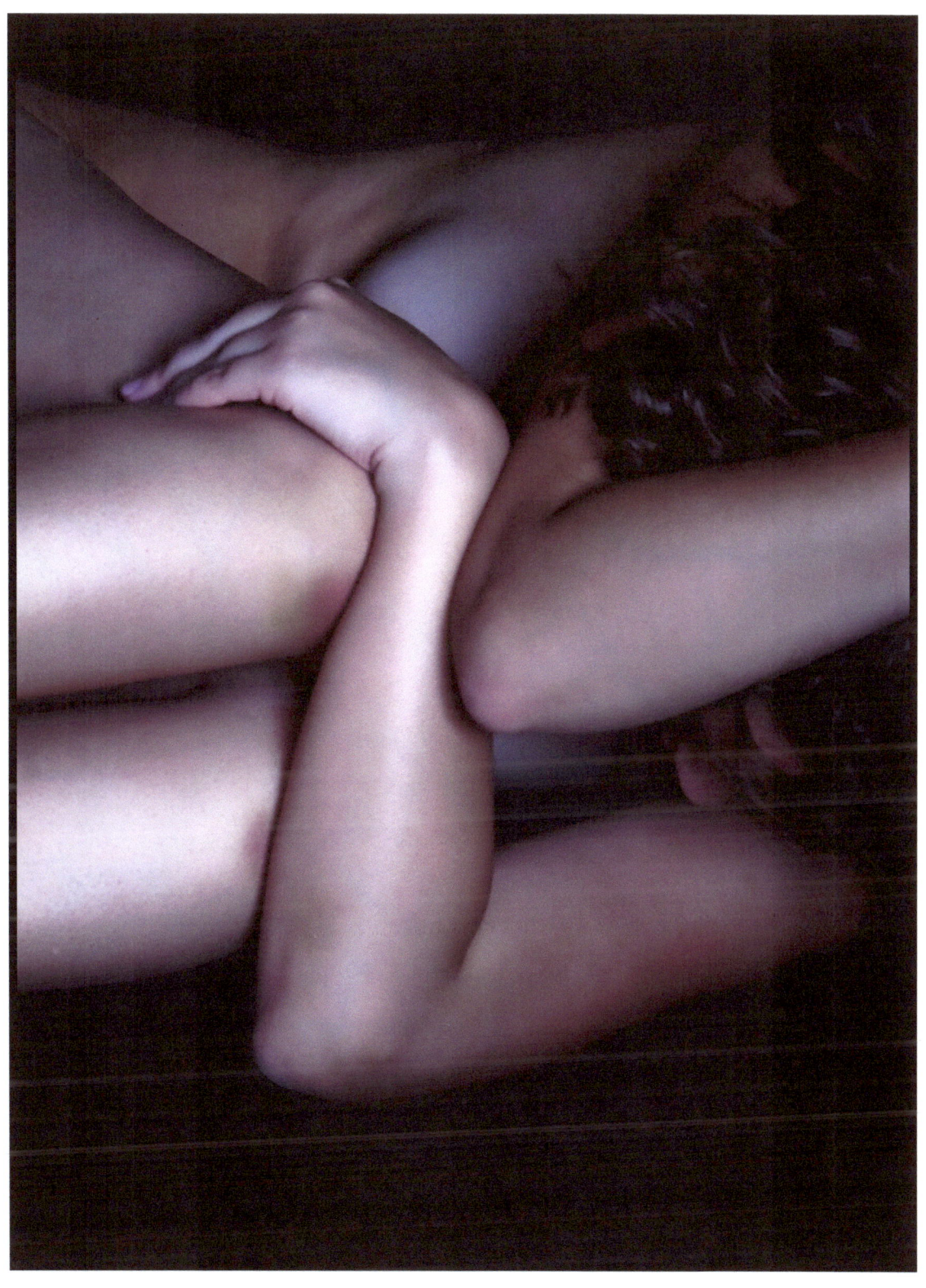

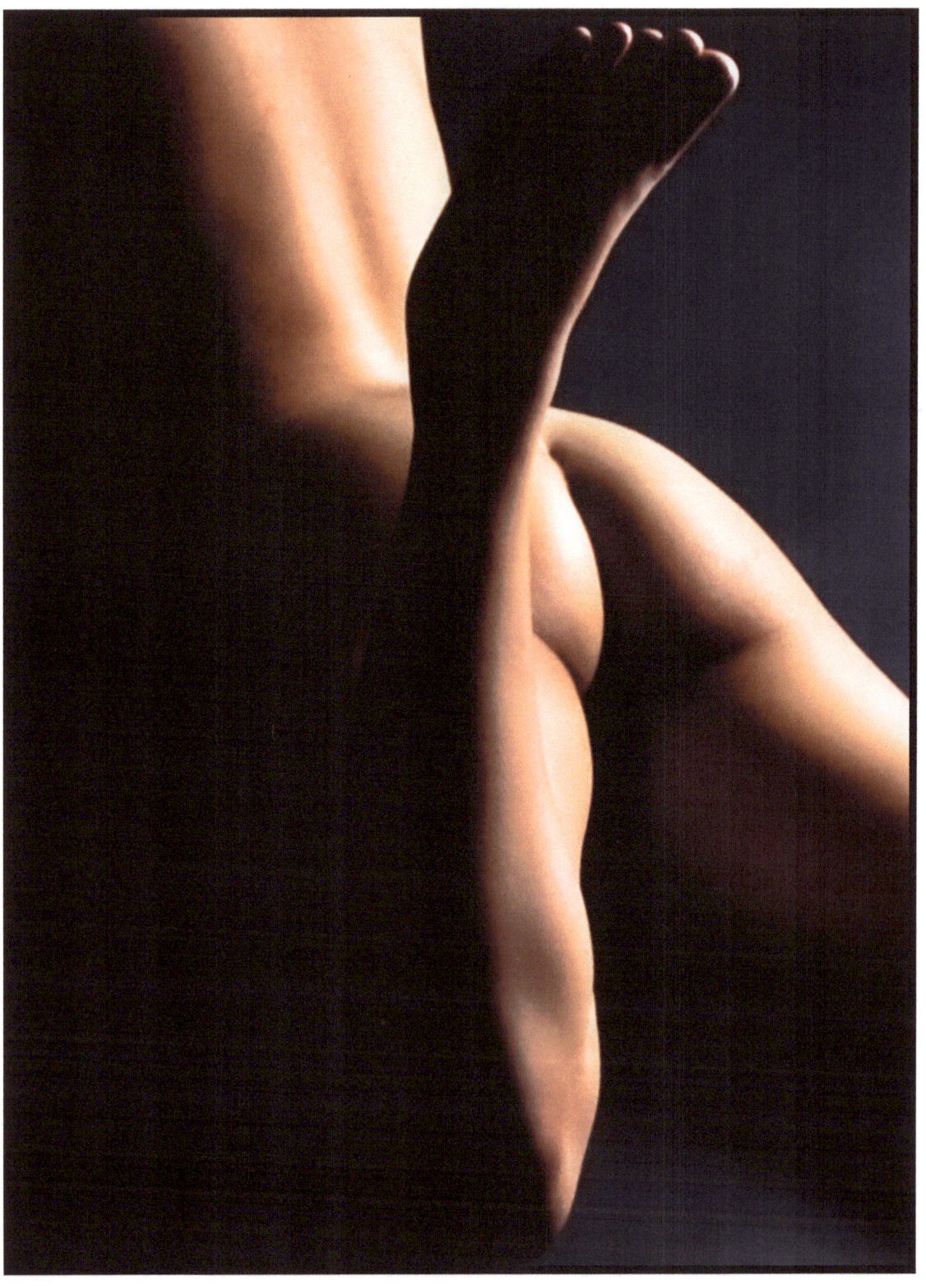

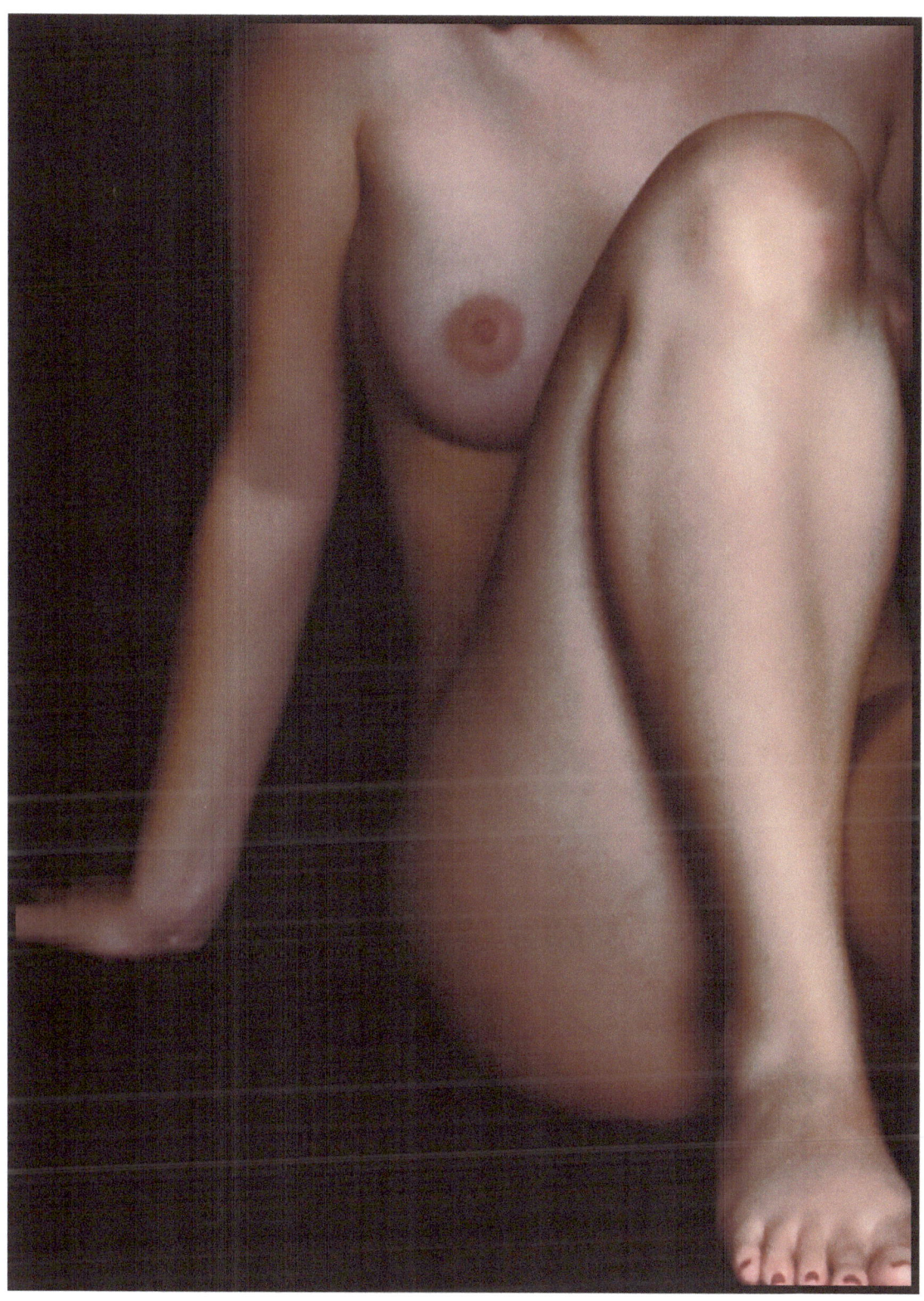

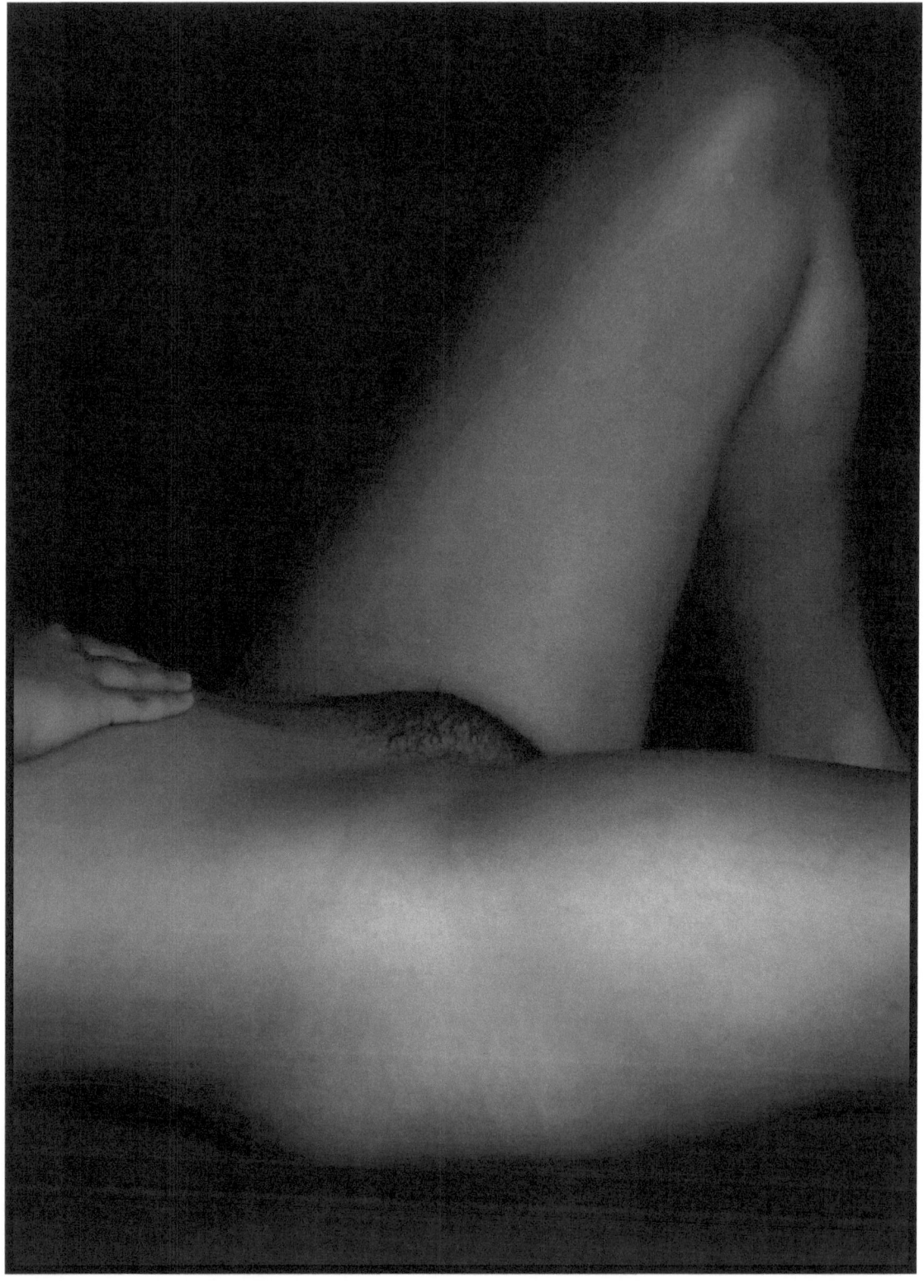

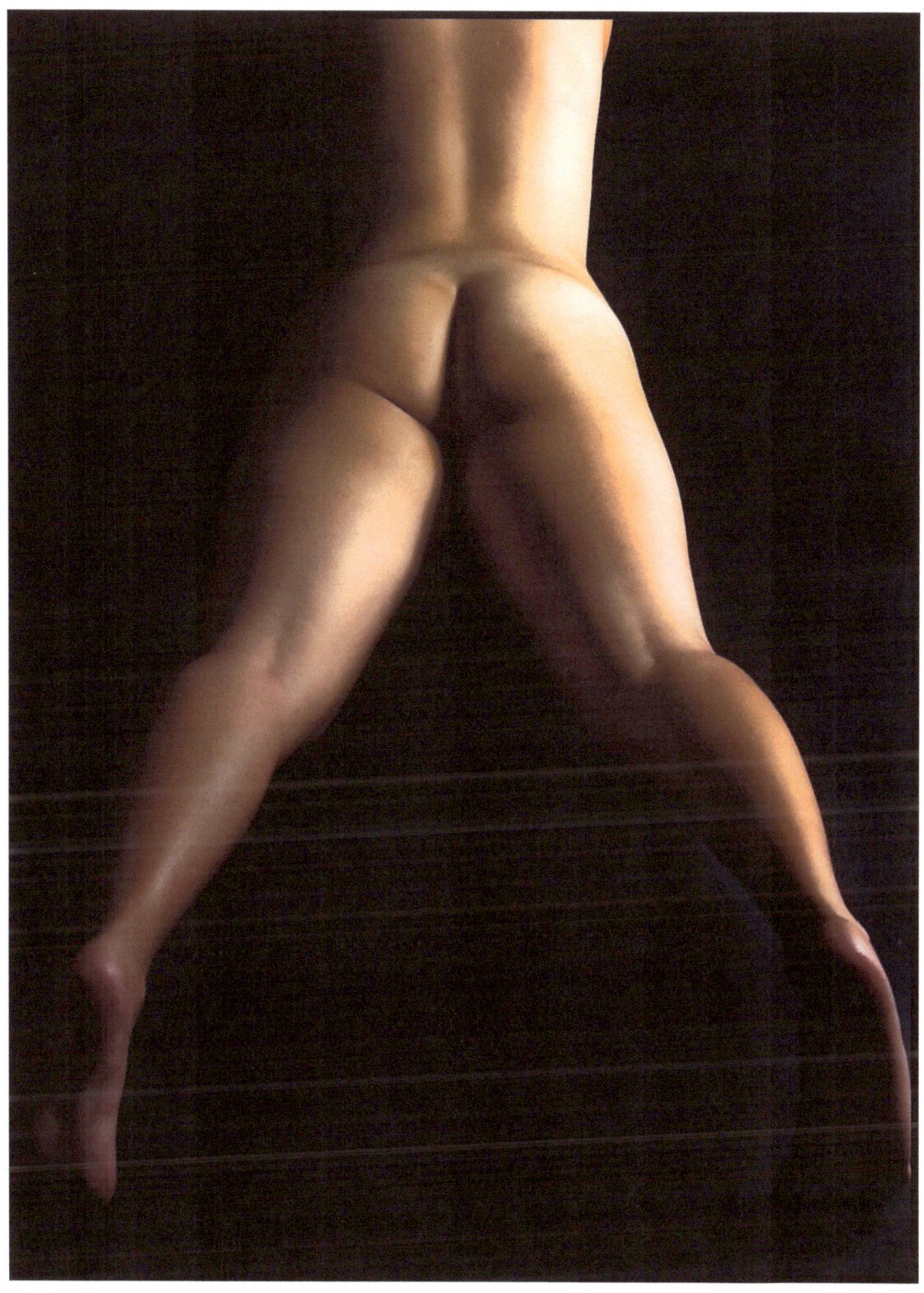

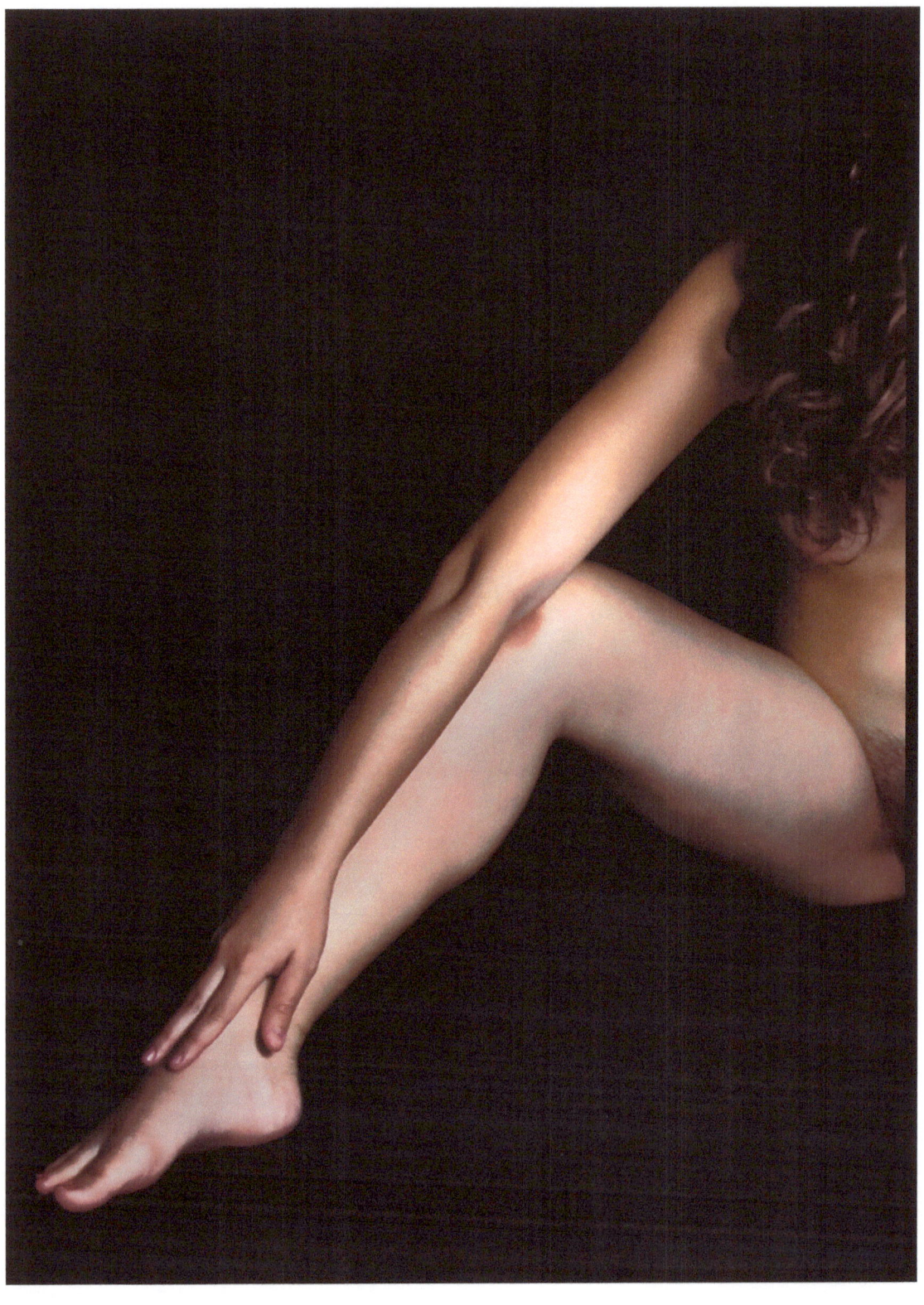

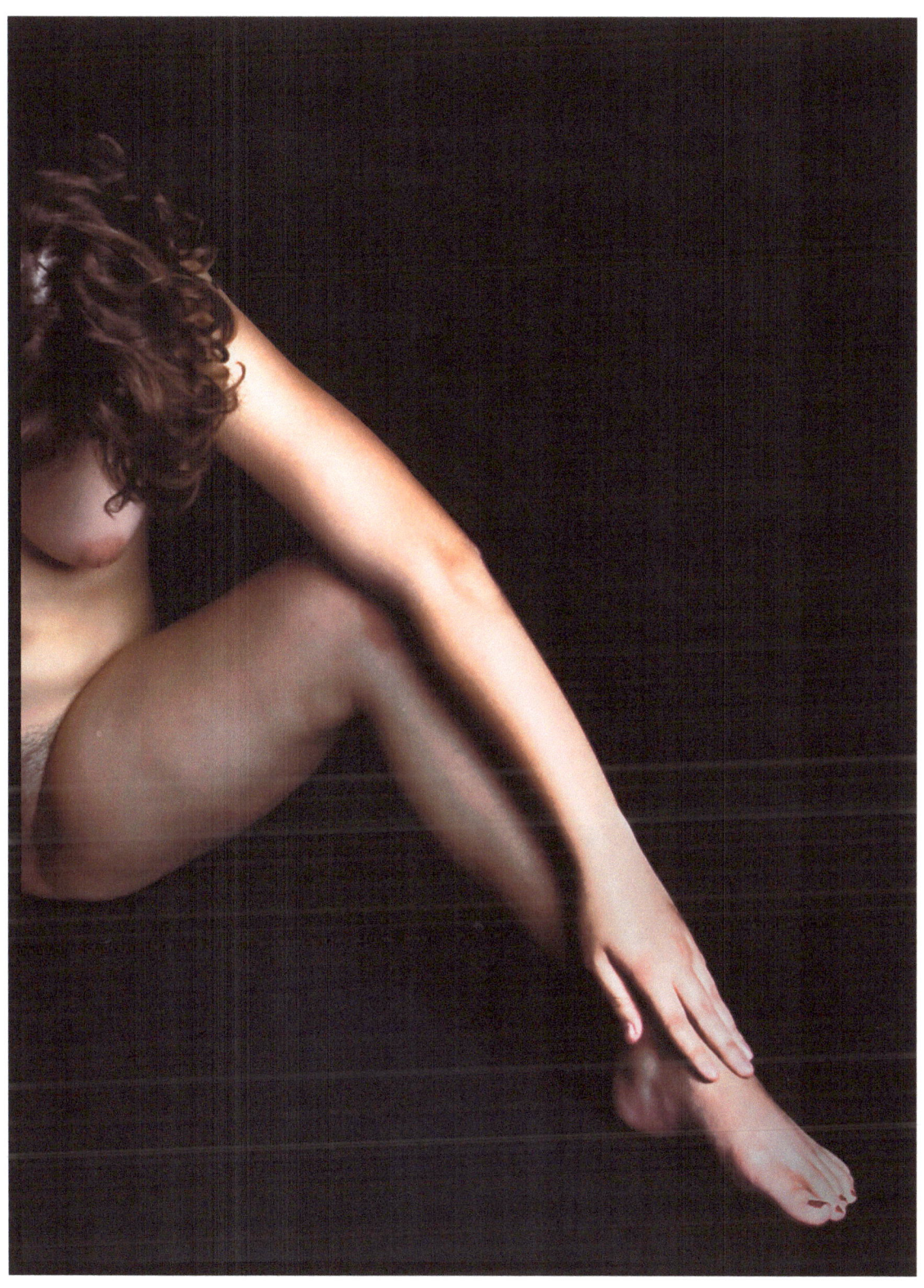

About the Author/Photographer

Born and raised in Dallas - Gary Melton is a Texan through and through. His journey into the world of photography began years ago with the purchase of a 35mm single lens reflex camera at a U.S. Army PX in Budingen, Germany.

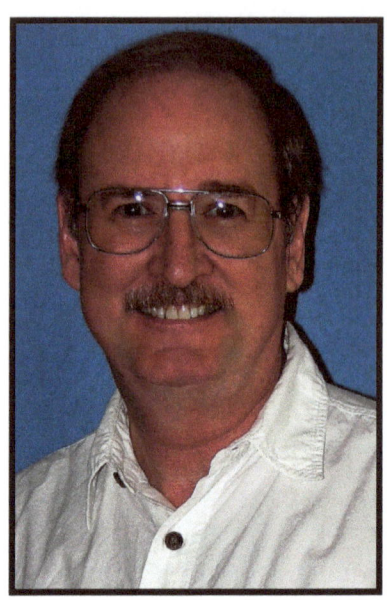

Shortly after leaving the service, what started as a hobby and grew into a passion, became an enterprise when he started a part-time portrait, team and event photography business. The magic of picture taking lost it's charm for him, though, when it became apparent that taking photos for money was a lot more about business than it was about art, so he closed the business after a couple of years.

Flash forward a couple of decades when he decided to re-new his passion, but in a different direction that he felt sure would be more interesting - female figure photography. He was right, and he was also a natural at it. It took a while to make the transition from film to pro-level digital, and it also took some time learning to find the necessary artistic con-nections with his models - but as I think you'll see, it was worth the time and effort spent.

Other books by Gary Melton:

Visions of Beauty: *12 Figure Models Captured*
Visions of Beauty II: *Images of 12 Figure Models*
Nine Women Revealed: *Intimate Revelations of Nine Real Women in Images and Words*

Quick Order Form

Fax Orders: 1-888-308-0462

Telephone Orders: 1-888-308-0462

Email Orders: orders@goofyrooster-publishing.com

Postal Orders: Goofy Rooster Publishing   PO Box 2904   Wylie, TX 75098-2904

Please send the following books. I understand that I may return any of them for a full refund - for any reason, no questions asked.

_____

_____

_____

Name: _____

Address: _____

City: _____   State: _____   Zip: _____

Telephone: _____

Email address: _____

Sales Tax: Please add 8.25% for products shipped to Texas addresses

Shipping/handling (US addresses only):

USPS Media Mail (2 - 8 days)   Add - $5.00

USPS Priority Mail (2 days)   Add - $8.50

[above rates subject to change as postal/shipping rates change]

www.ingramcontent.com/pod-product-compliance
Lightning Source LLC
Chambersburg PA
CBHW050841180526
45159CB00004B/1991